# AFRICA, AMERICA AND CENTRAL ASIA:

## Formal and Informal Empire in the Nineteenth Century

Edited by Peter Morris

EXETER STUDIES IN HISTORY No.9

Published by the University of Exeter 1984

# EXETER STUDIES IN HISTORY

## Editorial Committee

Prof I.A. Roots  MA FSA FRHistS
M. Duffy  MA DPhil FRHistS   M.D.D. Newitt  BA PhD FRHistS
C.D.H. Jones  BA DPhil FRHistS   B.J. Orme  BA MPhil FSA

## Publications

No 1  The Military Revolution and the State 1500-1800
edited by Michael Duffy   (Price  £1.75)

No 2  Government, Party and People in Nazi Germany
edited by Jeremy Noakes   (Price  £1.75)

No 3  'Into Another Mould': Aspects of the Interregnum
edited by Ivan Roots   (Price  £1.75)

No 4  Problems and Case Studies in Archaeological Dating
edited by Bryony Orme   (Price  £3.00)

No 5  Britain and Revolutionary France: Conflict, Subversion and
Propaganda   edited by Colin Jones   (Price  £1.75)

No 6  Nazism 1919-1945  Vol 1  The Rise to Power 1919-1934
edited by J.Noakes and G.Pridham   (Price  £2.95)

No 7  Roman Political Life 218 BC - AD 69
edited by Peter Wiseman  (forthcoming)

No 8  Nazism 1919-1945  Vol 2  State, Economy and Society 1933-1939
edited by J.Noakes and G.Pridham   (Price  £5.75)

Printed in Great Britain by A. Wheaton & Co. Ltd., Exeter

ISBN 0 85989 295 6
ISSN 0260-8626

# Contents

# Acknowledgements

The contributions to this volume were first presented in the form of papers to a one-day conference on 'Territorial Expansion versus Spheres of Influence', held at the University of Exeter on 4 July 1984. The organisers would like to thank the participants, who came from SOAS, LSE, Lampeter, Bristol, Queen's College Cambridge, the College of St Mark and St John Plymouth, and Plymouth College of Further Education as well as from various departments within the University. Their helpful comments have greatly benefited the resulting papers herein contained. The Editor would especially like to express his appreciation to Hilary Tolley for her help in preparing the text for publication, and Mike Rouillard who drew the maps and designed the cover.

The Editor

# Introduction

## PETER MORRIS

Under the impact of the First World War Lenin, then in exile
in Zurich, wrote a short pamphlet entitled Imperialism, the Highest
Stage of Capitalism.(1)   Arguably his most widely read work, it
reflected the then current certainty that the late nineteenth century
had seen the emergence of a 'new' imperialism, arising from economic
causes.    This view had a profound effect on emerging Third World
nationalism.    Thirty-five years later, in the aftermath of the Second
World War, British and French empires rapidly disintegrated.    Whilst
Lenin's view of a world completely shared out between international
capitalist monopolies in conflict with each other, leaving war as the
only means of redistribution between them, continued to hold sway in the
Soviet Union, historians elsewhere began to re-assess the predominantly
economic interpretation of imperialism and to question whether the
latter was as 'new' as hitherto claimed.    The process began in Britain
with the publication of Gallagher and Robinson's article 'The
Imperialism of Free Trade' in 1953, later elaborated in Africa and the
Victorians (2), in which they argued that it was much less novel than
previously suggested, and developed a concept of 'informal' empire which
has been very influential subsequently.    The four papers in this little
volume are   a modest contribution to the continuing debate and cover
aspects of the subject sometimes overlooked.

The wide differences between the areas covered and the
processes by which they were 'imperialised' illustrate the problems of
definition and timespan which have bedevilled much theoretical writing
on the subject.    In one sense it may be questioned whether there was
anything new and distinctive about the later nineteenth century process.
As three of the papers show, there was a marked continuity from earlier
periods and little sign of a sharp and readily identifiable break in an
ongoing process.    Late nineteenth century developments formed part of

the ebb and flow of empire, as charted by amongst others Koebner and Lichtheim.(3) In another it may be argued that neither the Russian nor the American cases here examined formed part of the imperialist process, as indeed the governments of both firmly state. Like treason, imperialism is perhaps only so to be described when unsuccessful, dead and gone or at least clearly moribund. Moreover the dividing line between wicked imperialism and laudable territorial expansion is, by any standard, thin. Spreading overland is obviously different from spreading overseas and the former has been viewed with greater indulgence than the latter. Was the onward spread of Imperial Russia into Asia imperialism or a continuation of the process by which the old Grand Duchy of Muscovy had evolved? If the khanates of central Asia and the steppe lands of the kirgiz were indeed colonies, presumably the lands of the erstwhile principality of Kazan were too, not to mention those occupied by Lithuanians, Estonians and Letts which were forcibly re-absorbed into the Soviet Union in 1939 as part of the Nazi-Soviet Pact, forming one of the few examples of 're-imperialising' whereby former colonial possessions having once secured their independence are re-absorbed. Similar considerations apply to the United States, whose colonising activities began long before the U.S. took an interest in overseas territories. Like Russia, the United States was the product of an expanding frontier spreading over a continent. American thrusts west into the sparsely populated lands of the mid- and far west had obvious parallels with the Russian thrust into Siberia. The wagon-trains and land-hungry settlers enjoyed the support of the firepower, mobility, commissariat and organisation of the U.S. cavalry and the latter heaped up the corpses of native peoples desperately resisting invasion. In that respect they closely resembled Russian, British and French armies in colonial wars. In one important respect American ruthlessness was greater, for the indigenous inhabitants did not survive to lay claim to separate national status, to a national homeland or to enjoy the benefits of president Wilson's commitment to national self-determination as seconded by Lenin after 1918. The two successful empires which survived into the second half of the twentieth century were those which sponsored the demand for subject peoples elsewhere to determine their own future, whilst denying that that principle had any applicability to their own states. Imperialism has therefore come to mean expansion overseas and the exercise of domination over a foreign people numerous enough to object and to make its voice heard.

Domination came, as it always had, in many different forms. The most obvious was formal empire, the assertion of political control over an area and the imposition of the full panoply of governors and administrators, backed by armed force. It may also have been the least successful and most short-lived. As Malyn Newitt's paper on southern Africa shows, it was often a last resort, taken only when other, less expensive measures failed. Much depended on what came afterward. Most imperial powers tried hard to secure the wholehearted consent of at least a part of their new subjects, for preference the old ruling elites whose power was permitted to continue and who became surrogate members of the ruling race. That was the British approach in India, the Russian in central Asia and the Portuguese in Africa. The enthusiasm of African chiefs for top-hats and tail coats, the outward symbols of the power and majesty of the new rulers, were no curious cultural aberration but indications of the success of imperial powers in absorbing the old rulers of their new possessions. Habibullah, amir of Afghanistan and client ruler of British India, preferred Rolls-Royces and pianos. Members of the ruling families of central Asian muslim khanates or kirgiz nomads proudly wore Russian decorations and held colonelcies in tsarist regiments whilst American Indian chiefs took to the bowler and armchairs. Imitation in these cases was the sincerest form of flattery, and it was carefully fostered. In the U.S., winning over traditional rulers was less important for settlers were flooding into tribal lands. Something similar happened in South America as incoming southern Europeans progressively Europeanised the continent. In comparison the small numbers of settlers who went to Africa or central Asia before 1914 made little impact on the vastly larger native populations. To be really permanent imperialism required heavy colonisation, the secret of U.S. and later Soviet success. Indeed, land-hunger characterised the steady onward flow of each until it encountered either the ocean or a people sufficiently numerous to halt it. As Benjamin Franklin put it, a ruler who 'acquires New Territory, if he finds it vacant, or removes the Natives to give his own People Room' deserves the gratitude of posterity.(4)

Given the superiority and ruthlessness of imperialists it made sense for ruling elites to throw in their lot with them. Their positions might indeed be strengthened thereby, as Colin Lewis and Peter Morris show in their respective papers. From the stand-point of subsequent generations of nationalists anxious to rid themselves of the foreign yoke (and to insert themselves into the resulting power vacuum) such behaviour was treasonable, but in the pre-modern Third World the imperial conqueror who left his new subjects unmolested in the enjoyment of their property and old ways of life and secure in their traditional social and political relationships was greatly to be preferred to the conqueror who massacred and pillaged in the style of Gengiz Khan, Cortes or Pizarro. Collaboration might be unheroic but it was sensible, as many found in Nazi-occupied Europe. The consequence of this symbiotic relationship between outside imperial power and native governing class was to make nationalist movements politically radical, as much opposed to their own traditional rulers as to the dominance of foreigners. It was easy to assume that nationalists were radical reformers. Once in power they usually showed themselves to be nothing of the sort. It explained however the attractiveness of Lenin's analysis and gave some plausibility to the easy identification of nationalists with communists. Particularly appealing to U.S. policymakers, whose easy dismissal of any suggestion that their own activities were imperialistic is examined by Joseph Smith, the result was often to make theory into reality, as the evolution of Castro's Cuba showed.

By far the most satisfactory form of imperial relationship from the point of view of the imperialising power was the informal one by which subjects of the latter secured advantages without their states incurring the expenses of annexation. These could be very heavy. Russia's central Asian territories never generated adequate tax revenues before 1914 to recoup military and administrative outlays. It may be doubted whether the revenues from her African possessions covered British governmental expenses there. The South American solution was ideal. As Colin Lewis's paper illustrates, the cooperation of local elites and the freedom permitted foreign capital investment and the repatriation of profits met the requirements of British, Americans and others. The occasional military demonstration and pressure to secure prompt payment of outstanding interest did not begin to compare with the expenses of wars against Boers, African peoples, Afghans, nomadic tribesmen or decaying Spanish armies and fleets. If late nineteenth century capitalism made any distinctive contribution to the imperialism of its day it was this preference for informal penetration. By contrast proponents of direct annexation and control were by and large drawn from the older landed and professional classes who had always dominated government and thought in terms of rule, not profit. A proper empire in their view required ostrich plumes and military governors. Healthy national balance sheets kept buoyant by the inflow of profits from foreign investments or from the industries which processed colonial raw materials or from the sales of manufactured goods required a sophisticated modern outlook rather uncommon amongst the decision makers of late nineteenth century Europe. Of the two remaining world empires their present-day characteristics reflect rather closely the very different ways in which they were created: the Soviet reflects the pre-modern, pre-capitalist formal annexatory style, the U.S. the dominance of capitalist, informal ways.

The pressure groups which urged on their respective governments' imperial activities were an interesting mixture of 'old' motives for expansion typified by military and official circles and 'new' ones of freebooters and adventurers, no longer the sixteenth century conquistador or privateer but their modern descendants. Individual private citizens with the firepower, mobility and organisational skills of the modern world were often more than a match for native societies. Their self-confidence and self-righteousness were accordingly enhanced. The new marginal men were unable to make quick careers in increasingly ordered metropolitan societies with little free land, well developed financial and economic structures and restrictions on individual activities. To get rich quick, actually or metaphorically, they needed an outlet. Many found their way to the United States. The patriotic however preferred to find their land of opportunity under the protection of their own flags, modestly anticipating the possibility of rapid personal advance into the ranks of the governing elites of their own states. It was this aspect of their ambition which often made them prickly subjects for their governments to control – a Skobelev, Rhodes or Marshall. Some were economic speculators, as Malyn Newitt shows. Many were not.

Amongst the earliest analysts of the 'new imperialism' was J.A. Hobson, whose Imperialism, first published in 1902, remains one of the classic texts. Echoing Adam Smith's strictures on mercantilism a century and a half earlier, he identified the essentially sectional nature of the advantages brought by colonies, noting that their acquisition meant great gains for rather small groups

> the business interests of the nation as a whole
> are subordinated to those of certain sectional
> interests that usurp control of the national
> resources and use them for their private gain.(5)

Like Lenin, he focused attention on economic gain. Yet as the papers of Newitt, Morris and Smith demonstrate there were other forms of gain. Soldiers of humble origin anxious for the rapid promotion unobtainable in an age of peace between the powers could secure it in colonial wars.

Missionaries anxious to save souls found an almost unlimited supply amongst pagan tribesmen. Administrators secured niches for themselves with considerably better material rewards than they would have secured at home. Like administrators everywhere they ensured eminently satisfactory pensions. Explorers sought the support of their home publics whilst indulging their private interests and gave vicarious excitement to armchair-bound members of Geographical Societies. The latter urged the necessity of making discoveries before other nations whilst arguing the international character of science. The Société de Géographie was founded in Paris in 1825, its Berlin counterpart in 1827 and the Royal Geographical Society in 1830. Russia, behindhand in this as in other aspects of modernity, had to wait until 1845. The map of the world was littered with physical features newly discovered for Europeans and Americans, and provided with outlandish names - Lake Victoria, the Bismarck Archipelago, Mount Kaufman, the Alexander chain, the river Roosevelt.

The popularity of imperialism ought not to be underestimated. As Edward Said has shown(6), it might be attributed in part to escapism from the unfamiliar and often disagreeable world of modern industry. Empire allowed men to be men and old verities to be re-affirmed. Such sentiments were most appealing to the old ruling elites whose domestic political as well as economic dominance was in decline. As the men on the spot also enjoyed a monopoly of information, as true in Africa and central Asia as it was in Venezuela or on the north west frontier, their reports and advice guided the decisions of their home governments.(7) For generations of British public-school boys, educated in the values of an old, rural and patriarchical world of noblesse oblige and deference it must have been refreshing to find black men who accepted the myth of their effortless superiority at a time when the lower orders at home were turning to leaders from their own ranks whilst the commercial and industrial classes regarded public administration and law-giving, those mysteries monopolised by the lengthily and expensively educated, as little more than out-door relief for an indigent upper class. There was of course an ebb and flow of public interest and colonial reverses could and did ruin political careers such as those of Ferry and Crispi, but these were untypical cases. Overall it buttressed the domestic status quo, at least in the short term.

That was, no doubt, why it was so very unpopular with political radicals such as Hobson or Lenin. Imperialism fortified the existing order and won votes for conservatives from new mass electorates. As armies gathered and fleets sailed the home public could read accounts of triumph and thrill with indignation at the savagery of lesser breeds without the law. In that sense there is some truth in the argument that imperial conquests formed an alternative to war between the powers, for it had the effect of welding national cohesion and papering over class strains. That this consideration should have had such a wide impact was however new. In no previous epoch had so many potentially imperialising powers existed simultaneously as they did in the later nineteenth century, possessing to a greater or lesser degree the necessary material power. They all claimed to play their part in the general European civilising mission, and indeed the divine allocation of functions within that general framework to individual nations had been part and parcel of the theories of nationalistic writers such as Mazzini and Schleiermacher. To radicals prone to knowing, unromantic and hard-headed views of human behaviour the only explanation for this was the development of capitalism and the elaboration of a conspiracy theory. Yet that is almost certainly too restricted an explanation of a phenomenon which enjoyed such widespread currency.

Whatever the explanation of the growth of the imperial urge in the colonising states may be, as Malyn Newitt and Colin Lewis both show, the development of the international economy continued regardless of it and drew wider and wider regions of the world into a common economic unit. The process was independent of individual action or intention, and for marxists is proof of the iron laws of economic determinism. It is impossible to date the beginning of the process. Trade and the exchange of goods involves profit and loss, or exploitation of the weaker partner by the stronger, and always has. The use of force to secure precious raw materials had long been an historical reality. Developments in the southern African economies were clearly fortuitous in the sense that they were never intentionally devised and had a momentum of their own. They also generated further opportunities and openings into which yet more newcomers stepped. The history of the international economy, which perhaps began with the ancient Greeks, has continued into the era of the multinational corporation. For a brief period at the end of the nineteenth and start of the twentieth centuries governments were universally convinced of the necessity to secure empires. Even those with no record of imperial activity, such as Sweden or Switzerland, were active in securing contracts with governments of 'backward' states by which their nationals were employed as expert advisers, the case for example with Swedish officers in the Iranian gendarmerie. That they did so was a reflection of the dominant motif of the age, which, despite the proud language and jaunty symbolism, was fear.

In an hitherto unparalleled era of change and opportunity each and every imperial power believed itself under mounting threat, its economic well-being threatened by predatory neighbours and its citizens losing out in the universal scramble to take advantage of the oportunities offered by the decline of the old empires of Spain, Portugal and Holland, of Ottomanns, Iran and China, as well as by the impersonal forces of modern capitalism. Thus it was the specific issue of Spanish decline which touched off U.S. extra-continental imperialism in 1898, the theme of Joseph Smith's paper. Russian governmental anxieties about the economic decline of the Empire, British concern lest other states' empires institute 'closed door' economic policies shutting out British goods, and British pressures on South American states in the interests of free trade were parallelled by French, German and Italian demands. In the latter two the taste for state-building and frontier-drawing had been only recently acquired. Such fearfulness was disguised in the language of moral obloquy. For Americans the imperialism of British and Germans was immoral and their own annexations in fact liberations of native peoples, a view still suprisingly widely held. Precisely the reverse view was held in Britain and Germany. All imperialising powers denigrated others whilst congratulating themselves in the most laudatory language. For Russians the 1857 uprising in India expressed the true feelings of oppressed natives who, were Russian troops to approach her frontiers, would rise in exultation at impending liberation. Soviet historians have taken over the argument in toto.

For the British, German rule over native peoples was synonymous with all that was evil.

Beneath the rhetoric lay solid enough economic considerations. The steady inroads of the world economy dominated by the industrialised powers, had serious consequences for the economic life of the imperialised regions. As Colin Lewis' contribution illustrates, there is often no consensus as to the nature and consequences of the process: local conditions, political as well as economic and social, could produce very different results, even within the confines of a region subject to the same process. Local economies were however confronted with major problems. The reality of mono-culture was dangerous dependence on a single crop, be it coffee or rubber or cotton, with all its disruptive consequences and the threat to local populations if that crop ceased to be needed by importing industrialised economies or if the compensating flow of food imports was disrupted. Local handicraft industries collapsed under the impact of imports of mass produced factory manufactures. Old social systems disintegrated as their economic bases were undermined. None of this depended on formal empires being established and it was a virtually universal experience. Local, native economies and societies would never be the same again.

The process was reinforced by the construction of new engineering works. Hydraulic works, whether for irrigation or drainage, canals and railways not only required large sums of capital leading to demands for the safeguarding of the investment but were seen by governments as objects requiring protection, as the examples of the Suez and Panama canals proved. These works of communication were permanent and their existence subtly influenced international economic developments as well as the local host economies. They offered new sources of revenue for local economies, new opportunities for entre-preneurship both local and foreign, new employment with concomitant effects on the local labour market and distorted the traditional trade routes with on-going repercussions for local economies. Whilst often beneficial, such fruits of industrial development were not always advantageous for they could ignore the realities of local conditions. Malyn Newitt's observations on the ecological impact of railways in southern Africa has parallels in central Asia where the uprooting of saxaul plants for fuel for the railway engines greatly decreased the stability of desert sands. Yet the framework of many political units which have now gelled into modern nation states was provided by railway lines and water works. It was not only Canada which fitted the definition of a railway in search of a country.

Not surprisingly the process was often self-perpetuating. Acquisition of one colony led easily to the argument that its defence against military aggression required points d'appui and coaling stations, against disorder necessitated the taming of uncontrolled tribesmen beyond the frontier whose native governments were unable or unwilling to do the job themselves. Measures were urged against natural catastrophe arising from water shortages (the argument for controlling the headwaters of the Nile and even for finding out where they were) or against shortages of raw materials, an argument very apparent in the debate over oil supplies on the eve of the First World War. All imperial powers were persuaded to accept the argument in one form or another thus incurring additional expense, arousing patriotic emotions and assisting the sectional concerns of interested parties.

Whether it makes much sense to separate out one element and accord it the title of prime mover may well be questioned. Imperialism was a very complex and continuing process whose all-pervading nature is clear. Yet there was a sense in which it was 'new', for the tempo and dimensions greatly expanded after the mid nineteenth century. Whether this reflected the development of capitalism, the search for new markets for manufactured goods, the ever-increasing provision of raw materials for manufacturing industries and the need for profitable outlets for investment capital which could not be profitably absorbed in the industrialised economies remains a matter of debate. Besides those contained in Peter Morris's contribution, there were many other examples of reluctant capitalists who had to be pressed into taking advantage of what governments saw as the opportunities offered by colonies. At best it is a partial explanation, more satisfactory in its application to notions of 'informal' empire than to the formal assumption of control and establishment of colonies. Indeed, as Malyn Newitt shows the argument has to be stood on its head so far as Portuguese colonies were concerned. Perhaps it is least applicable to the process by which millions of Europeans left for distant continents. All too often they went in search of land, that most pre-capitalist of commodities, and represented surplus populations which would otherwise have provided metropolitan industries with still cheaper labour supplies. To that extent this process may well have represented anti-capitalist economic forces. Yet it would be unwise to reject it out of hand for there clearly were instances where the development of modern capitalism was relevant, as was the case in South America. Perhaps it is wrong to see the process as everywhere and in all respects the same. Different impulses toward empire-building may well have coexisted, some looking back, others forward and reflecting the astonishing variety of social, economic and political structures to be found in late nineteenth century Europe and America.

## Notes

1.  V.I. Lenin, Imperialism, the Highest Stage of Capitalism (Petrograd, 1917).

2.  J. Gallagher and R. Robinson, 'The Imperialism of Free Trade', Economic History Review 2nd ser., 6, 1953, pp.1-15 and Africa and the Victorians (London, 1961).

3.  R. Koebner, Imperialism (Cambridge, 1961): R. Koebner and H.D. Schmitt, Imperialism, a Political Word 1840-1960 (Cambridge, 1964); G. Lichtheim, Imperialism (London, 1971).

4.  Cit. Lichtheim, op.cit., p.57.

5.  J.A. Hobson, Imperialism, a study (3rd edit., London, 1968), p.46.

6.  E.W. Said, Orientalism (New York, 1978).

7.  M.E. Yapp, Strategies of British India (Oxford, 1980).

# Latin America from Independence to Dependence

## COLIN LEWIS

Debt crises, protracted negotiations with the International Monetary Fund, bloodshed in Central America, the rising force of popular protest, malnutrition, the harsh fact of increasing inequality and the divergent fortunes of various military regimes all contribute to the image of Latin America during the early 1980s. Those events reinforce long-held popular perceptions of the continent as a region of instability, of poverty and of turmoil, subject to recurrent foreign intervention. Latin America, it is alleged, lacks political institutions capable of resolving class conflicts and sectional antagonisms without recourse to violence or appeals to external forces. The prevalence of these views and the enduring image of social and political tensions upon which they are founded compels a closer examination of the continent's relations with the outside world. For if in Britain, parts of Europe and the United States of America a stereotype view of Latin America prevails — as a continent of endemic authoritarian military oppression and economic mismanagement (or worse, chaos) — some Latin Americans and others would maintain that the realities which underlie poor economic performance, social decomposition and institutional fragmentation result from the nature of the external connection. Current processes represent the culmination of an unequal relationship between Latin America and the north Atlantic world conceived at the time of the Iberian conquest during the sixteenth century and perpetuated by subsequent asymmetrical commercial and financial relations.

The pessimism which pervades the gloomy economicism of many journalistic commentaries in English upon the present predicament of the continent is in marked contrast to aspirations engendered by the struggles for freedom from Spain and Portugal. The countries of Latin America secured their independence between 1808 and 1826: the Napoleonic invasion of the Iberian peninsula was the immediate cause of the revolutions for independence. The timing, course and consequence of the wars of independence are now major points of disagreement in the controversy about the external connection. For some writers, the countries of the continent indeed threw off the yoke of European control during the early decades of the nineteenth century. National identities were forged in the heat of the revolutionary upheaval and former colonies emerged as sovereign states co-equal with countries of the Old World and a newly-independent United States. The collapse of the

Iberian empires in Latin America, which had been many decades in the making, facilitated, for other authors, a more vigorous penetration by Britain during the late nineteenth and early twentieth centuries – the classic age of imperialism.  For yet another group of scholars, however, the classic age of Latin America's colonial exploitation has been the palpable dependence of the continent upon the United States since the Second World War, a dependence that was already observable during the inter-war decades and emerged from a pre-1914 US challenge to British hegemony in parts of the region.  Hence the legacy of several centuries of colonial exploitation by Spain and Portugal was a subsequent dependence first on Great Britain and later on the United States that frustrated the formation of a dynamic economy and inhibited political maturity thereby giving the lie to independence and to possibilities of national sovereignty.

In addressing the debates about imperialism and dependence this essay will focus upon the century following independence.  The period encompases the decades immediately after the struggles with Spain and Portugal which many regard as critical in the formation of state structures, and the years of remarkable (and for some, self-sustaining) expansion following the 1860s and 1870s, when the area was more effectively incorporated within a world economic system that, by dint of her commercial, financial and naval supremacy, was focussed upon Britain.  This periodisation underlines the peculiar position of Latin America in the discussions elaborated in this volume.  As the continent was not reconquered by Spain or Portugal and remained (at least nominally) independent, the debate hinges upon the nature of institutional arrangements, the determinants of policy, and patterns of Latin American expansion.  Were state structures congruent with endogenous requirements?  Was policy responsive to a variety of domestic interests?  Did economic growth promote development and autonomy or was it merely a vicarious byproduct of a distorted pattern of domestic resource utilisation determined by external forces?  For lack of space this essay will not deal with the post-1920s period which, some scholars have argued, witnessed the consolidation of US corporate dominance facilitated by increased financial power, growing military might and the willingness of successive US administrations to intervene overtly or covertly in the internal affairs of the Latin American republics.

1.   Independence: Illusion or Reality?

Traditional scholarship has long recognised the frustration and unrealised expectations associated with the half-century following the 1820s.  Great stress – probably an over-emphasis – was placed upon the heroic scale of the struggles for independence in the orthodox historiography which deals with Spanish America.  Much of this literature projects the political rather than the economic. Administrative reforms during the late eighteenth century destroyed a complex set of relationships between the colonial bureaucratic and military establishments, on the one hand, and the upper echelons of colonial society on the other.  The rupture between newly-appointed colonial administrators and Americans was heightened by the exclusion of criollos (whites born in the Americas) from offices in state and church which the local elites had customarily regarded as their perquisites. Further cleavages resulted from slights – real or imagined – suffered by the colonial aristocracy at the hands of peninsular officials whom the former regarded as socially inferior. An ideological dimension to weakening ties between Spain and Empire was provided by the circulation of the ideas of the Enlightenment in the colonies and subsequently by the success of British North American colonies in obtaining their freedom and the example of revolutionary France. Thus the process of Spanish American independence was depicted as a clash between moribund, reactionary Spain and colonies revolutionised by new ideas of political and social organisation, enhanced by creole alienation.(1) The resultant struggle was both protracted and severe during which successor institutions were slow to emerge. The collapse of legitimacy in the Spanish colonies initiated a process of disintegration and intermittent warfare during which opposing influences competed for ascendancy. Following the wars of independence conservatives challenged liberals and those favouring a centralised state challenged interests wedded to looser federalist arrangements. By implication, such scholarship accepts that the process of political decomposition following independence may have resulted in complications with foreign powers.

Many aspects of this traditional approach have been disputed in the recent literature. If it had long been recognised that the disintegration of Portuguese-Brazilian links was a more muted - and indeed a more complex - process, modern writing is also inclined to present Spanish American independence less in terms of a simple clash between criollos and peninsulares and more as a civil war that saw a broad spectrum of similar ethnic and social groupings aligned on both sides of the struggle.(2) While creoles constituted the core of the movements for independence, many remained loyal to the Spanish crown or only threw in their lot with the rebels when the withdrawal of Spain from South America was final or inevitable. Both insurgent and royal forces attempted to conscript slaves or to recruit Indians, mestizos and pardos (mixed races) into their ranks. Modern scholarship also emphasises the potency of localism and regional antagonism rather than ideology in post-independence societies riven by faction.

Yet in one important respect traditional orthodoxy and revisionist writings are in agreement. Both point to the weakness of the state apparatus during the half-century following independence and thus to a possible lack of competence in handling relations with foreign powers. For traditionalists the flight of peninsular officials reduced administrative efficiency in the new nations and undermined the positive role of government in securing order. Newer scholarship points to post-independence internecine struggles as a function of the fragmentation of the elite which, raising the spectre of social revolution, engendered elite fears and deflected attention from the need to confront new forces of imperialism.

Much of the traditional historiography lacked an economic dimension, though some scholars referred to the role of (mainly foreign) merchants - essentially as agents promoting the circulation of new ideas rather than as social actors representing a dynamic challenge to a decrepit ancien regime.(3) For some this was principally another aspect of the ideological causes of the struggle against Iberia. By the end of the eighteenth century laissez-faire concepts threatened mercantilist precepts as effectively as the Enlightenment challenged accepted views of government. Contraband trade (a forceful precursor of free trade) undermined a colonial system founded upon monopoly and exclusion. An economically dynamic Britain was as compelling an example to frustrated criollos as the newly independent United States or France at the time of the Revolution. Direct discussion of the economic dimension is to be found in writing which develops the fiscal and financial aspects of late-colonial attempts at reform. Pombaline measures designed to nationalise the Portuguese-Brazilian economy, although a pale shadow of their Hispanic counterparts (the Bourbon reforms) were, like them, motivated by a perception of metropolitan decline which could only be reversed through colonial regeneration.(4) If Spain's position in Europe was to be retrieved, it could only be as the result of greater efficiency in imperial administration and an efficacious application of policies designed to promote colonial expansion.

Yet the very successes of these programmes resulted in the disintegration of empire and perhaps initiated more subtle forms of dominance. Increased metropolitan intervention in areas of the economy hitherto the preserve of creoles antagonised colonials when economic expansion was accompanied by an exponential increase in the burden of taxation. Improved levels of economic activity and related growth of commerce made the Spanish Indies an even more desirable prize to European (and also North American) rivals, especially Britain who was strategically well-placed in the West Indies to challenge Spanish attempts to revitalise colonial trade and had already established in Brazil a massive entrepôt from which to penetrate southern outposts of Spain's empire in the Americas. The rising volume of specie remitted from the Indies to Spain after the mid-1770s was eloquent proof of the effectiveness of reform and of the significance of the empire to Spain.(5) It also evidenced the exploitative nature of the links between mother country and colonies and contributed to the growing disaffection of colonials. Moreover, the widening commercial imbalance in imperial legal trade demonstrated the economic disintegration of the colonial compact. Spain, in the face of a growing volume of colonial exports, was unable to produce the goods demanded by empire which increasingly turned to contraband to satisfy the demand for imports or resorted (with varying degrees of success) to domestic manufacture despite imperial proscriptions to the contrary. Indeed, by 1800, the theory of colonial complementarity had been displaced by the practice of imperial competition. Spain and her colonies competed for access to foreign markets: Spain and Spanish America strove to sustain a flow of imports from the same European and North American suppliers. For disgruntled criollos, the burden of empire was compounded when direct contraband trade revealed the true costs of a restrictive colonial commercial monopoly which, in theory at least, required that all imports be supplied via Spain even when the mother country was herself incapable of manufacturing those products. By this stage the benefits of empire were less clear when, notwithstanding the vast amount of colonial treasure expended upon imperial defence, shipping lanes could not be kept open during late eighteenth century wars and colonial ports were prey to enemy attacks.

By this stage too, a number of fiscal changes designed to enhance colonial finances were regarded with growing apprehension by some sectors of society in the Indies. The removal of petty restrictions on persons of colour, the issuance - for a suitable fee - of certificates of whiteness to people of mixed race which enabled the holder to pursue a career in the professions were viewed at best as a

dangerous and inappropriate financial expedient or worse as a crude
device to encourage racial antagonisms so as better to preserve Spanish
colonial rule.(6)

Several of these issues surfaced during the revolutions for
independence and again in post-independence decades and have been
elaborated in the literature. How do divergent interpretations of the
process of independence, the aftermath of the Spanish American
revolutions and the collapse of Portuguese influence in Brazil, relate
to the nature of the post-1820s external nexus? For scholars of an
earlier generation, the disintegration of European empires in the New
World marked the end of the 'old imperialism' characterised by
mercantilist philosophies of exclusion and privilege, of state
regulation and monopoly. The old empires had emerged as the result of
European dynastic rivalries and economic systems that stressed commerce
before production and viewed international trade as a zero sum game in
which one nation's gain was another's loss. The motive for colonial
expansion had been the creation of self-sufficient units the better able
to accumulate bullion (in modern parlance, balance of trade surpluses)
which conferred strength upon the accumulating economy and implied a
consequential decline of competing powers.(7) The collapse of the old
empires was signalled by the independence of American colonies
(commencing with British North America) and was associated inter alia
with the industrial revolution in England and a transition from
commercial to industrial capitalism.

Thus for a number of writers the greater part of
the nineteenth century was a non-imperial age or even an interlude of
anti-imperialism. Outmoded monopoly mercantilist concepts were replaced
by a dynamic approach to international economic relations. This
approach was based upon the concept of laissez-faire. It was a form of
political economy that advocated a minimal role for the state and
emphasised an international division of labour. Individual initiative
and competitive capitalism, it was alleged, yield the greatest utility
for the greatest number. Free movement of goods and people rendered
colonies unnecessary. Imperial defense was in any case expensive,
occasioning higher levels of taxation than would otherwise have been
required and thus constituted an illiberal intervention in the rational
individual's ability to allocate capital so as to maximise economic
opportunities. Empire affronted liberal sentiments: it infringed
individual freedoms, was associated with monopolistic practices and
compelled the state to inappropriate action in the economy – all
anathema to liberals. Moreover, empire was linked with groups and
political interests opposed to dynamic industrialists, namely
traditional landed sectors, engrossing middlemen who sought monopoly
commercial privilege in order to dominate producers, and so forth.

In the Latin American literature the basic problem addressed
was the means by which newly-independent countries should avail
themselves of the opportunities provided by anti-imperialism and an
expanding international economy. It was patently obvious that the
period following the break with Spain and Portugal was not one during
which expectations aroused by independence were realised. Various
explanations are available. Given its emphasis upon the political, the
focus of traditional writing was directly upon institutional collapse
and enduring instability during the early national period. Although not

explicitly concerned with the poor economic performance of the republics during the second quarter of the nineteenth century, orthodox scholarship offers some insights into the problems of the period. The collapse of central authority in most areas, the oscillating fortunes of war (which produced a cycle of royalist/insurgent ascendancies), the balkanisation of Spanish America and associated recrudescent civil strife, are sufficient explanation for many. Pursuing this line of analysis, others have argued that the cathartic effects of independece struggles and post-independence rivalries produced in the countries of Latin-America a tabula rasa upon which new ideas of social and political organisation were inscribed, engendering distinct institutional and governmental frameworks which were only consolidated in the 1860s and 1870s. These original arrangements ultimately secured national objectives and facilitated the realisation of the aims of independence - economic progress, social harmony and a status for the countries of Latin America which was equal to that of European nations and the United States.

Associated with the traditionalist approach, though a minor element in the school, was the work of those scholars who related poor performance at independence, and subsequent slow pace of autonomous expansion, to specific factors. Pointing to the traumatic effects of the struggles for independence and accepting the heroic scale and devastating consequences of the military campaigns, these authors referred to economic dislocation.(8) They argued that the upheavals disrupted internal and overseas trade routes which were difficult or impossible to re-establish in the smaller fragmented adminstrative units that emerged by the 1870s. War distorted or destroyed productive resources: mines were flooded and could not be drained because of inadequate technology; cattle were slaughtered and stock not easily regenerated. All sectors of the economy suffered from a scarcity of labour: Indian workers abandoned the mines, slaves were recruited into the armies and militias from plantations and urban workshops. The enlistment of slaves, whether killed in battle or liberated on completion of military service, represented a capital loss to former owners. Spanish and Portuguese merchants repatriated capital and their expulsion from the continent also meant a loss of entrepreneurship. Floods of imports destroyed what artisanal manufacturing capacity survived. Continuing instability, scarcity of money and sharp periodic changes in commercial codes and tariff regimes did not facilitate recovery. A further strand in this approach disputed whether the countries of Latin America possessed a mix of resources appropriate for development. Absorbing a factor-endowment view of expansion, popularised in early discussions about the causes of the industrial revolution in England, these writers argued that, at a time when rapid progress was associated with an industrial revolution based upon steam power, the republics could hardly be expected to industrialise when they did not possess adequate exploitable deposits of iron ore or coal.

Additional economic explanations for the lack of progress manifest during the half-century following independence were to emerge later from the structuralist view of development elaborated within the Economic Commission for Latin America (Comisión Económica para América Latina) an agency of the United Nations Organisation. Founded in 1948, ECLA (CEPAL) produced during the 1950s various studies of the post-Second World War Latin American predicament. Its observations and methods of analysis were quickly absorbed by scholars who sought an historical dimension to those post-war problems. Structuralists rejected a supply-push view of development, favouring instead a Keynesian demand-pull explanation. For scholars of this persuasion, lack of progress during the period studied was to be explained in terms of institutional deficiencies and structural defects. Small populations, the predominance of subsistence activities, limited absorption of modern technology, capital scarcity and an inadequate infrastructure constrained potential for growth. Problems of market integration and low levels of productivity were compounded by an ineffective state apparatus and/or the adoption of economic policies that were not congruent with national requirements.(9)

## 2. The Challenge of Dependency

From the above it is clear that these analyses of the post-independence decades and beyond were more concerned with issues pertaining to political stability and economic growth than problems of imperialism. Yet these approaches produced a response from scholars who address directly the question of imperialism in Latin America. Purporting to apply a Marxist interpretation to the study of Latin America's relations with the outside world, A.G. Frank challenged conventional interpretations of independence and disputed also neo-classical assumptions implicit in the historical component of cepalista analysis. He argued that the lack of economic progress in the region following independence, and subsequent distorted patterns of activity during the nineteenth century, was the result of capitalist penetration of the continent dating from the time of the Iberian conquest.(10) Contributing first to the dependency debate and later writing more precisely within the world-system framework, Frank elaborated the concept of 'metropolis-satellite' relationships in order both to interpret the course of Latin American history since the sixteenth century and examine the mechanics of external connection. He claimed that chains of dependence linked Latin American societies to metropolitan economies and facilitated a flow of the surplus, in the form of capital, from the latter to the former. The development of the centres was predicated upon an ability to extract surplus profits from the periphery which was accordingly rendered not backward but underdeveloped - a dynamic retrogressive condition that increased, rather than merely perpetuated, the development gap between centre and periphery.

Frank challenged two orthodoxies. First in asserting that the Latin American economies were underdeveloping, he spurned classical theories of growth which maintained that backward states could best develop through progressive incorporation into the world economy. Conventional liberal concepts of growth had stressed that the dynamic international system which emerged in the latter part of the nineteenth century provided less advanced regions with an opportunity to overcome domestic constraints to growth. Factor flows - in the shape of immigrants and foreign investment - facilitated the supply of resources essential for development. Indeed, after the United States, the Argentine and Brazil were the principal beneficiaries of the massive movements of people from the Old World to the New which occurred between the 1860s and the 1920s. Participation in world trade meant access to elements - technology and capital goods - not readily available domestically.  Openings to foreign markets provided Latin American countries with a means of valorising resources that would have yielded little return if utilised only within the confines of the domestic economy.  The insertion of Latin America into the world system after the 1860s was productivity-raising and profit-generating.  Frank rejected all this.  As stated above, he maintained that Latin America had been effectively incorporated into the world capitalist system in the sixteenth century: the region's connections were not revitalised during the latter part of the nineteenth century.  Plunder in the conquest period was replaced by exploitative investment - firstly in mining, agriculture and commerce, subsequently in loans to government and in the infrastructure.  External dominance of key sectors ensured extraction of the surplus. Foreign investment in railways, ports and utilities enhanced the export configuration and anti-industry bias of economic activity.  High-interest loans to governments perpetuated indebtedness and sustained in power a small elite which depended upon external forces to secure its position in confrontations with other domestic groups. These were the sinews of metropolitan domination and Latin American underdevelopment.  Only when links with the outside world were severed - as for example during the First World War - could Latin America develop.

Secondly, Frank challenged Marxist orthodoxy concerning the progressive nature of capitalism as an agent provoking social conflict. Acknowledging his debt to US Marxist scholarship, he pointed to changes both in the metropolis and satellite.  Consequently, although capitalist modes of production had existed in Latin America since the conquest, the colonial status of the region endured as metropolitan capitalism adjusted the mechanisms of dominance.  In part, following the Steins (11), Frank held that while the continent was nominally part of the Spanish and Portuguese empires until the 1820s, Iberia itself had long before been reduced to semi-colonial status by countries north of the Pyrenees, notably Britain - a status that was institutionalised by such devices as the 1703 Methuen Treaty between Britain and Portugal.  Latin America passed from formal Iberian colonial territory to dependence upon Britain during the period of free trade and to a condition of exploitation by US transnational corporate capital during the latter part of the twentieth century.

From this perspective, the weak political arrangements that emerged at the time of independence and poor economic performance during the early national period were indeed related phenomena.  However, they did not facilitate the subsequent dominance of Latin American polities by Britain, rather these phenomena were functions of the already dependent status of Latin America.  In this respect, early contributors to the dependency debate inverted the causality and also the chronology elaborated in the traditional historiography about Britain's position in the republics during the nineteenth century.


## 3. Order and Progress: the Internal Dimension

Frank's concern to demonstrate the endurance of the external linkage echoed an earlier hypothesis of Gallagher and Robinson, though it is not clear whether he was fully aware of their writing.  From their study of Britain and Africa during the Victorian heyday, Gallagher and

Robinson formulated the concept of <u>laissez-faire</u> imperialism or imperialism of free trade.(12) In a seminal article drawing heavily on the Latin-American experience they rejected the assumption that an anti-imperial interregnum had existed between the 'old' and the 'new' imperialism (the latter typified by the scramble for Africa and Great Power pressure upon China during the late nineteenth century). They also detected a clear quest for paramountcy in British foreign policy during this period which gave added force to the drive to imperialise. Drawing upon Lenin and Hobson, Gallagher and Robinson located the impetus for imperialism in the advanced capitalist economies. They also accepted the Leninist position of acute capitalist rivalry during the age of high imperialism – hence a British concern for primacy in markets like Latin America. The generalities of this approach were later refined by Robinson who ascribed a vital role to collaborative elites within regions subject to enduring or resurgent imperialism. For Gallagher and Robinson the character, composition and expectations of Latin American elites explain why the continent was not formally re-colonised following independence. If, as related, they followed Hobson and others in accepting that the drive to imperialise emanated form the central economies, they allocated to the periphery the determination of the nature (and possibly the timing) of the imperial connection. Throughout the nineteenth century British policy in Latin America and elsewhere was dominion by '...informal means if possible, or by formal annexations when necessary...'(13), the determining factor being the reaction of local elites to British requirements and objectives.

Formal empire-building was time-consuming, troublesome and expensive: it was to be avoided if at all possible. In as much as Britain's prime concern during the nineteenth century was access to markets, secure sources of raw material and food supply and possibly outlets for the investments upon which commercial expansion depended, imperial policy was determined by the need to ensure an environment favourable to the expansion of commerce. Where political instability threatened to disrupt commerce or an established domestic interest sought to discourage overseas trade, Britain colonised. Where local elites welcomed commercial and financial links with Britain, informal means sufficed as Britain's naval supremacy and competitive edge secured hegemony. This was not to project local elites as supine agents of British imperialism. On the contrary, these groups could only perform an appropriate role if sufficiently established to defend their position against other domestic interests opposed to class links with Britain or who threatened, for whatever reason, the peaceful order upon which international specialisation and exchange depended.(14)

Britain's objectives in Latin America were assured when landowners, government officials and others endorsed policies of free trade. Indeed, during the decades following independence many South American republics were more wedded to <u>laissez-faire</u> principles than was Britain, where the last vestiges of mercantilism were not removed until the mid-nineteenth century. Thus Britain's dealings with the republics were typified by the negotiation of treaties of amity and commerce which stressed reciprocity and equal treatment without favour. Only exceptionally, in the case of Brazil, was London anxious to obtain preferential terms. Thereafter policy consisted of facilitating free navigation on international waterways and pre-empting regional conflicts or domestic instability that might hinder trade. Hence the use of good offices to secure the independence of Uruguay in 1828 which prevented a damaging Argentinian-Brazilian struggle over the east bank of the River Plate, and the denial of recognition to the province of Buenos Aires during the 1850s when it attempted to secede from the Argentinian Confederation. Others have detected the long arm of the British Foreign Office in the war against Paraguay waged by the Argentine, Brazil and Uruguay between 1865 and 1870. A closed economy, Paraguay represented an autonomous alternative to liberal orthodoxy whose anti-free trade, interventionist government challenged the model of laissez-faire upon which British paramountcy depended.

Gallagher and Robinson's approach compels a focus upon the internal: it corrects an imbalance in the work of crude exponents of dependency such as Frank who are excessively concerned with external factors. Indeed, Frank has been subject to much criticism. His account of the course of Latin American history has been castigated by Marxists precisely because it ignores discussions of class, because it confuses a money economy (or the accumulation of capital) with capitalism, and above all because he diverges from Leninist orthodoxy. Non-Marxists have challenged his failure to differentiate adequately between substantive changes in the external connection over time, and have argued that he has been over-selective in the use of data and also that he has paid insufficient attention to the composition of national elites.(15) Hence the significance of the hypothesis advanced by Gallagher and Robinson, and more particularly by the major text produced by Cardoso and Faletto, which considers both the composition of national elites and provides a dynamic framework for the study of divergent Latin American cases.

In 1979 Cardoso and Faletto produced Dependency and Development in Latin America, a substantially revised and expanded version of the original Spanish edition published a decade earlier.(16) They paint a broad canvas upon which is depicted the detail of several centuries of Latin American history. The dialectical approach of Cardoso and Faletto provides a framework for the study of the continent's development that acknowledges sharp differences in national or regional experiences. At the core of their analysis is an investigation of the participation of endogenous groups in the process of accumulation. They identify three degrees of participation. The highest occurred in those areas where elite groups retained control of productive resources and preserved a large interest in ancillary activities such as primary product processing, commercialisation and transportation - sectors from which domestic entrepreneurs were able to launch forth into a greater diversity of profitable capitalist (particularly industrial) ventures. The lowest degree existed where national groups became marginalised, losing control of domestic resource elaboration, and played little role in associated activities, thereby limiting the spread effect of overseas trade within the host economy. An intermediate case existed when local dominant classes retained control of the means of production but played only a minor role outside the staple sector. In the late nineteenth and twentieth centuries Brazil, some Andean mineral exporting economies, and the River Plate republics respectively conformed to these three models. For these authors, the processes of economic and social change can only be understood by an analysis of the relationship between the internal and the external - a complex nexus of coincidence and coercion amongst external forces, domestic dominant classes and local dominated groups. The composition of this web of social and economic grouping was the key to the differentiated typology elaborated.

An examination of internal socio-economic structures and the scale of domestic participation in key activities yielded insights into the capacity of certain Latin-American economies to diversify and explained also the relative strength of specific elites. Extensive patterns of land usage, as in the Sao Paulo coffee zone, geared to supply a rapidly growing foreign market enjoyed particular advantages when the stock of fertile, cultivable land was virtually limitless. Rapid movements of the agricultural frontier and the topography of the coffee area required heavy investment in fixed capital projects - railways and distribution facilities - and implied an increasing demand for labour and a widening range of employment prospects in coffee production and ancillary activities. With the effective end of the trans-Atlantic slave trade in 1850 and of the internal slave trade by the late 1870s, coffee zone labour requirements could only be satisfied by immigration from Europe. The flood of Italian immigrants and the consequential substitution of free for slave labour resulted in the growth of a wage economy and the monetarisation of rural areas. A consolidation of the market created new opportunities for investment, notably in manufacturing, which attracted <u>fazendeiros'</u> (coffee planters') profits. The process, which diffusionists would attribute to the 'trickle down' effect of incomes generated in the export sector, was described by Cardoso and Faletto as associated or dependent development. Less progressive was the example provided by mining economies. A wasting asset, mineral deposits were often located in regions distant from historic centres of population concentration and administration. By the late nineteenth century non-ferrous metal ore extraction, and later oil production, depended upon an advanced technology that was not available in Latin-America. Capital intensive enterprises, the mining companies generated little demand for labour nor, given the technology gap, did they provide opportunities for domestic entrepreneurial initiatives. Mining concessions were consequently exploited by foreign rather than domestic capital. Geographically isolated, mineral producing enclaves were also more easily provisioned from abroad (the local market absorbed only a small proportion of total output) and were hardly integrated into the national economy. Profits flowed mainly to foreign investors, only a small proportion remaining in the host economy where it accrued to a narrowly circumscribed group composed of lawyers and political advisers employed by the corporations or state functionaries whose incomes were defrayed from minimal taxes levied upon mining enterprises. The domestic spin-off from these activities was severely limited: the manner of exploiting mineral resources did little to expand domestic demand or to foster market integration. Rather the process sustained sectoral, regional and income inequalities. Economies with an export sector dominated by mining activities were unlikely to achieve dynamic dependent development unless the government was capable of maintaining a high fiscal participation in corporate profits or export earnings. Indeed, <u>Dependency and Development</u> stressed the importance of the state apparatus in securing arrangements (both with domestic groups and foreign interests) conducive to endogenous accumulation.

Cardoso and Faletto's work (especially as subsequently refined by Cardoso) remains one of the most sophisticated and possibly most plausible explorations of the subject. A focus upon the social dimension rectifies the economicism of some early ECLA-inspired essays, but it must not be forgotten that the initial research for Dependency and Development was within the Commission. This framework – in its emphasis upon both endogenous structures and exogenous forces – constitutes a more comprehensive and comprehensible tool than crude dependency texts which proclaim that the proximate social revolution is the only solution to Latin America's problems or predict gloomily that the adaptability of international capitalism precludes dynamic social development. Observing that socialism is not on the immediate agenda and acknowledging that for all countries of Latin America the external connection has been and remains exploitative, they nevertheless postulate that it is possible to construct a dynamic national capitalism in certain countries.

Many aspects of this projection carry conviction: in several societies the popular and bourgeois heroes of Marxist revolution are weak or ignorant of their historic role. The proletariat is hardly large or homogenous. In the nineteenth century labour mobilisation was a painful and incomplete process. During the twentieth century urbanisation was based largely upon the expansion of tertiary activities rather than industrialisation. Both urban and rural labour proved difficult to organise. When a sizeable urban labour force emerged it was often co-opted and controlled by the state, as in Brazil and elsewhere during the 1930s. Middle classes were equally slow to emerge and even when relatively large, as in the Southern Cone (the Argentine, Chile and Uruguay), by 1914 were fragmented and dependent – composed in the main of professionals associated with export interests or government administration. Such groups sought to ape their betters; they did not pose a serious threat to the status quo. Elsewhere, industrial entrepreneurs were either of immigrant origin and aspired to acceptance by the elite or had emerged from the ranks of the landed aristocracy. These elements hardly constituted a challenge to the dominant classes as portrayed in Western Europe during the rise of industrial societies: they were part of the dominant sector. Cardoso and Faletto are correct when they dismiss the possibility of immediate social change in favour of readjustments and accommodations. If a dramatic realignment in external relationships presupposed a profound shift in Latin America's social structures, then limited modifications rather than a sharp rupture were to be expected.

4. Contemporary Opinions: Growth and Imperialism or Development and Autonomy?

While Frank typifies an early strand in the dependency approach, Dependency and Development a later, more refined school, and some cepalista writing yet another, an insufficiently recognised contribution are works produced within Latin America during the early twentieth century. These texts represent an original criticism of contemporary liberal economic orthodoxy. Like Cardoso and Faletto subsequently, these authors were concerned with the political economy of Latin American expansion. A number of scholars, particularly those writing during the inter-war years, addressed the question of imperialism directly. Some, notably those based in Buenos Aires and

Santiago de Chile, were exercised by the external vulnerability of their economies and the social and fiscal consequences of sharp contractions in levels of activity in the foreign trade sector. Several writers expressed alarm at the large involvment by foreign interests in key areas of the economy. A number wryly observed the continuing 'inferiority' of Latin American nations in spite of many decades of rapid economic expansion.(17)

Additional force was imparted to this literature by the effects of the First World War and the impact of the world depression of 1929-1936 (during which some commentators perceived increased levels of direct imperialist pressure). An ideological thrust to the debate was provided as a result of the 'discovery' of Marx and Lenin by Latin American intelligentsias: the works of Marx and Lenin only became widely available in translation during the inter-war period. However, this is probably to exaggerate the influence of such texts, and others by Hobson et al. Many radical re-evaluations of the continent's links with the outside world undertaken during this period were written from a perspective that would later be described as structuralist or possibly pre-Keynesian and owed much to an earlier Comtian tradition. Where analyses produced a prescription for change it was in terms of greater government action to promote economic diversification, or advocated attracting capital from a larger range of sources. In Mexico there were conscious attempts to place public bonds on European money markets so as to reduce reliance upon New York. There was also a pragmatic, and probably misplaced, Mexicanisation of the railway network. In the Argentine, US and French finance was welcomed as a counterbalance to what was viewed as an excessive dependence on Britain. Few contemporaries expressed alarm at the growth of US corporate investment in the republics at this juncture - a phase that later historians would mark as initiating a new form of dependence. Such policies - and their effectiveness may be questioned - were reformist not revolutionary. If ideologically motivated they owed more to nationalism than to Marxism-Leninism.

The scale of external influences in the republics was, however, real enough. Chilean nitrate production was dominated by foreign capital. One-third of Mexico's productive land was owned by aliens in 1910 and mining and petroleum areas were virtually foreign enclaves. Tropical and sub-tropical plantation agriculture in Central America, the Caribbean and elsewhere was almost exclusively the preserve of external capital: coffee in Brazil, Costa Rica and - of growing significance - Colombia was possibly the only exception. Exports were processed by companies that were registered abroad and increasingly operated in more than one Latin American centre of production. Overseas trade was almost exclusively carried in foreign bottoms and even coastal shipping and intra-continental trade was dominated by foreign flags. While in the Southern Cone there was a large domestic (not always state) presence in banking, foreign houses were also significant. Further north, commercial banking and merchant banking were mainly in foreign hands. Although, by 1914, state enterprises accounted for approximately two-thirds of rail networks in Brazil, Mexico and Chile, construction had been financed by external borrowing. In the Argentine (which possessed the most extensive network in the continent) and Uruguay (which had the greatest density of track) similar proportions were accounted for by British-owned companies. In 1913 foreign investment

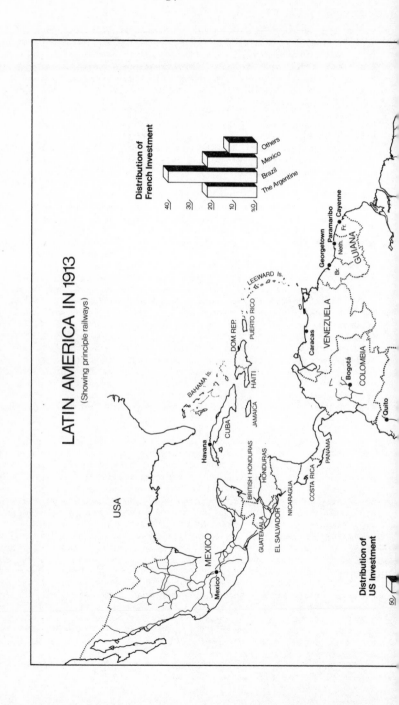

LATIN AMERICA IN 1913
(Showing principle railways)

Distribution of
French Investment

Distribution of
US Investment

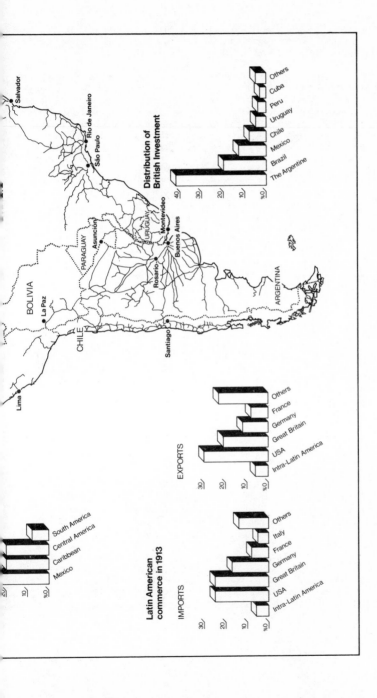

**Distribution of British Investment**

The Argentine
Brazil
Mexico
Chile
Uruguay
Peru
Cuba
Others

EXPORTS

Intra-Latin America
USA
Great Britain
Germany
France
Others

**Latin American commerce in 1913**

IMPORTS

Intra-Latin America
USA
Great Britain
Germany
France
Italy
Others

Mexico
Caribbean
Central America
South America

represented about one-half of total fixed capital stock in the Argentine. Throughout the continent immigrants and/or foreign companies were well represented in manufacturing.

Then, as now, this situation was portrayed as epitomising the colonial status of the continent. Although they would not have employed the term in its modern context, some Latin American policy-makers and intellectuals expressed concern about the dangers of unbalanced growth. Weakening prices for exports in addition to sharp annual fluctuations in foreign exchange earnings were known to result from increased competition in world markets. Low elasticities of demand for some tropical commodities and unresponsiveness on the supply side for others due to structural factors or the nature of the growing cycle aggravated the problem. The internal consequences of secular changes in world demand for these and other commodities was considerable given the predominance of primary products in export schedules. Levels of activity in the foreign trade sector directly influenced government revenue which consisted mainly of the yield on import and export tariffs. Personal incomes also depended on the buoyancy of the external sector to a greater or lesser degree. An index of the social cost of economic instability was provided by the incidence of banditry in some countries and the frequency with which the military was called upon to repress violent urban and rural protest in others.

Not all manifestations of 'colonial exploitation', then or since, were regarded as economic. Precursive of a later dominant strand in right-wing nationalist thought was the fear that - in those societies which received large numbers of immigrants - Hispanic cultural values were being distorted. It became fashionable to portray Italian and Spanish migrants as infecting native labour with socialist or anarcho-syndicalist ideas that destroyed natural, paternalistic, time-honoured relationships. Elements of the elite were depicted as flirting with Anglo-Saxon semi-democratic, semi-representative political arrangements ill-suited to Latin American requirements. Settlers were a potentially dangerous conduit for the transmission of alien values; a mechanism of imperialist penetration, they demonstrated a taste for imported goods and ideologies.(18)

5. Anti-Imperialism

This scenario - whether presented by early twentieth century Latin American pensadores or proponents of theories of imperialism and dependency - has been challenged, notably by D.C.M. Platt. Initially contributing to the imperialism of free trade debate, Platt later advanced the concept of business imperialism and finally confronted dependentistas.(19) Focusing upon the classic age of the 'new imperialism', his early studies drew substantially but not exclusively upon the experience of Latin America during the period of Britain's industrial and commercial leadership. Platt was indebted to the earlier work of H.S. Ferns, who had written upon the Anglo-Argentinian nineteenth century connection(20), and the general revival of anti-imperialism of free trade hypotheses prevalent during the 1960s. Platt and others reasserted the minimal role of the British government in promoting trade and finance which was in part ascribed to the disjuncture of business and state in Britain, a reflection of her ossifying primitive capitalism. Britain neither sought, nor achieved, a hegemonic position in the continent. Her role in Latin America was determined by the forces of competition and the rules of the market place. The late nineteenth century was a period of remarkable growth and related socio-economic change. Latin America's participation in a dynamic world economy, unfettered by mercantilist restriction and state intervention, resulted in substantial injections of capital and labour, of technology and entrepreneurship. In the circumstances the continent obtained the best deal possible from the international connection. For scholars of this persuasion, the concept of economic imperialism is outmoded and singularly inappropriate when applied to Latin America. In the light of recent empirical research, the discourse lacks the saliency and the currency it once enjoyed when vitalised by contributions from Hobson, Lenin, Luxemburg and Hilferding.

Considering the passive posture of the British government during the period, a 'business imperialism' framework was more attuned to the requirements of an investigation into the continent's relationships with external interests. Proponents of a theory of business imperialism identified three areas where evidence of foreign influence might be sought. First, foreign merchant interests could constrain the legitimate actions of a peripheral state by direct pressure, privileged knowledge or dissemination of an ill-suited ideology. Second, foreign business interests could suborn officials so as to blunt policies prejudicial to the external sector. Third, the mere presence of foreign business interests in the host economy could deny opportunities to domestic capital. Participants in the debate searched for evidence that foreign merchants and financiers had consciously attempted to control weak administration, or manipulated money markets so as to deny access to foreign capital to governments unresponsive to external demands while channelling funds to finance pliant regimes. The debate was concerned with the terms upon which Latin American governments floated public bonds abroad and the creation of monopolies by foreign groups - whether aimed at controlling public utilities or the cornering of markets or the dominance of productive capacity. Having examined the trades - from Brazilian coffee to Peruvian guano and West Coast iodine - they found little proof of enduring control or collusion. Commodity corners were notoriously unstable and generally short-lived. Utility companies, because they were natural monopolies, were subject to increased scrutiny during the nineteenth century. Responsive to the demands of consumers of railway and other utility services, governments resorted to nationalisation or regulation.

Shifting from a concern with the classical age of imperialism, Platt directed his attention at weak links in the chain of dependency elaborated by authors such as Frank. Their unilinear approach rested in part upon a claim that Britain attempted to achieve, and indeed obtained, a dominant commercial position in Latin America around the time of independence. This approach, argued Platt, was based upon an erroneous assumption of the importance of Latin American markets for Britain and an exaggerated view of the continent's overseas trade. Focussing upon the 1810s and 1820s, when either third markets were closed to Britain or Latin America had been starved of imports for many years, dependentistas were inclined to project a large immediate post-independence volume of overseas commercial and financial transactions into later relations with Britain. On the contrary, Platt maintained, once demand, pent up during the revolutionary wars, had been satisfied and the exigent financial requirements of the struggle for independence subsided, most republics disappeared over the edge of the periphery. The region was a marginal component of the early nineteenth century international economy of little or no interest to would-be imperialists.

Having long asserted that Britain's commercial presence in Latin America had been exaggerated - both at the time of independence and at the end of the nineteenth century when European and North American rivals forced British traders to seek softer markets in the dominions and colonies - most recently Platt has addressed the question of British overseas investment. His conclusions are that the estimates for the early nineteenth century and for the period of 'finance imperialism' must be severely revised downward. A substantial part of overseas government paper marketed in London was purchased by foreigners, often by nationals of issuing administrations. Public bonds quoted in sterling were preferred by citizens of many countries to series issued by their own governments at home in domestic currency. It was logical for the carioca rentière to purchase Brazilian public bonds underwritten by Rothschilds in London rather than those denominated in milréis available in Rio de Janeiro. Moreover, if Britons invested in utilities that operated in Latin America, domestic capital flowed into land, urban real estate and a range of city-based activities. For Platt, the focus of some exponents of theories of imperialism and dependence upon flows of finance directed from London towards the continent neglects an important national element in those flows and also underestimates the scale of capital available domestically and actually employed at home. Arguments about external dominance in Latin America predicated upon ill-founded assumptions about the scale of British investments in the republics must be reconsidered if the ownership of sterling assets is questioned and ratios of domestic to foreign finance revised.

Platt's essays on imperialism and dependence have provoked controversy. 'Cliometricians' have challenged his use of the statistics and indeed his competence to handle the data. Dependentistas and others argue that proponents of business imperialism are trapped within a particular conceptual ghetto. Over-concerned to identify direct state action or conscious attempts by businessmen to gain control of Latin American resources, they search for documentary evidence in company repositories that, given the informality of arrangements studied, is unlikely to exist. Critics also contend that even if Anglo-Latin American trade represented a relatively unimportant part of aggregate British commerce (and, itemising specific commodities or sub-periods, not all would accept that this was the case), the converse did not apply. Access to British manufactures and services was vital for the Latin American economies. While domestic capital may have been available, in key areas British finance and expertise was critical. Contemporary Latin Americans shaped their relationship with metropolitan government and business accordingly. In contrast, some scholars contend that Latin America required exposure to a more thorough-going imperialism, to an association with a more dynamic model of capitalism than that represented by early twentieth century Britain. Thus to minimise the scale of the British commercial and financial presence is to miss the point.

## 6. Definitions of an External Relationship

Where does the debate stand today? Is it possible to
construct a composite view from the disparate frameworks, hypotheses and
analyses that draw upon divergent methodologies and mutually
antagonistic ideologies? Since Lenin first referred to the Argentine in
his studies of imperialism or Gallagher and Robinson considered Latin
America during the high period of laissez-faire, it has been difficult
to sustain the view that territorial expansion constitutes the bedrock
of imperialism or that colonialism is exclusively associated with
military occupation and viceroys bedecked in ostrich plumes.
Nevertheless, given the language of the discourse, the obvious may be
stated. Following the collapse of Iberian authority in Latin America,
the region was not reconquered nor (with a few notable exceptions)
subject to prolonged occupation by foreign forces. Although Cuba and
Puerto Rico remained Spanish colonies until the end of the century, and
the Dominican Republic briefly sought to resurrect imperial ties with
Spain, it is difficult to portray foreign military interventions during
the nineteenth and twentieth centuries as attempts to reduce independent
states to the position of formal protectorates or colonies. Apart from
a few spectacular events – notably European involvement at the birth of
the short-lived Mexican empire of Maximilian and US actions in Central
America and the Caribbean – most military occupations of Latin American
territory were geographically circumscribed and of limited duration,
intended, for example, to protect foreign property during times of
insurrection or in response to the violation of diplomatic missions.
Occasionally Latin American administrations requested the landing of
small detachments of marines to protect foreign legations, recognising
that this was a mechanism to forestall possible future diplomatic
incidents. Cuba was clearly a case apart, but if Latin American
sovereignty was compromised, it was less as a result of military
occupations (of which there are numerous examples) than by other
factors.

During the struggles for independence the influence of
government was undermined, central administration lost power to the
regions or groups outside the state. Bureaucratic competence was
reduced by the flight of Iberian officials and was difficult to
reconstruct due to fissiparous tendencies within the elite that
heightened fears of social turmoil. In this respect Latin American
states were, by the early nineteenth century, ill-equipped to confront
the forces of imperialism. But the obvious weakness of the state in
Latin America at this juncture does not sustain an exaggerated
importance of its potential adversary. For much of the period the face
of international pressure was represented by the commercial house.
Foreign merchants did not always or inevitably enjoy the whip hand in
dealings with insecure – sometimes corrupt – governments. Platt is
probably correct when he states that Latin American countries required
little from the world economy during the decades immediately following
the revolutions against Spain and Portugal. Whether consciously
intended as such or not, a retreat into self-sufficiency was perfectly
feasible, and was an option exercised by various groups.

The picture during the classical age of imperialism is more
intricate. Indeed the debate itself is more complex, the literature
more nuanced. At some time during the last third of the nineteenth

century most Latin American countries were drawn (or propelled) into a closer interaction with the world economy. For some polities the process reinforced the dominance of anti-progressive forces; a number were locked into a mono-crop export relationship with the world market that induced in the host state a sequence of geographically and chronologically specific growth enclaves that inhibited national integration and did not promote development. Elsewhere different patterns may be observed. Access to foreign credit permitted the modernisation of infrastructure which, even when incomplete, strengthened the authority of the central state and facilitated national consolidation. After the 1880s, the Argentine displayed a remarkable capacity to diversify and expand exports. Following the War of the Pacific (1879-1883), Chile became excessively dependent upon the nitrate sector to provide both export earnings and generate government revenue but Peru, by the end of the century, had broadened her mix of exports and for some decades at least maximised domestic participation in income flows generated by the foreign trade sector.

If industrial expansion may be taken as an indication of an ability to contruct a national capitalism within the framework of expanding international capitalism, there were some real achievements by 1914. A shift in import profiles reflected these developments. In the 1870s, consumer goods - principally foodstuffs and textiles - had constituted approximately 90% of the Argentine'e imports, by 1912 capital goods and intermediate products represented over 60%. For Brazil and Mexico during the latter year the proportions for these categories were 43% and 33% respectively. By 1914 approximately 40% of the Argentine's demand for manufactures was satisfied by domestic production. Admittedly local industries produced mainly non-durables - the food sector was the largest - and often depended upon imported inputs. On the eve of hostilities in Europe, Brazil's shoe, flour and cotton textile industries supplied virtually the whole of local demand for these products. Indeed, the Brazilian cotton textile industry ranked tenth largest in the world by 1913. Various industrial materials and some capital goods were also produced domestically. For several authors the process of industrialisation sponsored by the expansion of exports during this period indicates increased Latin American autonomy, vindicating modernisation theory and sustaining arguments of anti-imperialism. The expansion of these activities at least refutes the charge contained in simplistic dependency accounts that export-promoting insertion within the world economy fostered the emergence of a virulent and successful anti-industry lobby in all countries.

Possibly of more importance than statistics portraying the growth of industrial investment or increased manufactured output in the continent is evidence of a more pragmatic and more self-assured approach to external relations on the part of Latin Americans by the end of the nineteenth century. Discussions referred to above about the large presence of external interests in key sectors of the economy and the perception of a growing dichotomy between Latin America and the advanced countries of the north Atlantic (notwithstanding a period of sustained rapid expansion enjoyed by some countries) was intensified by bouts of instability in the external sector. Spectacular exogenous shocks such as the Baring crisis, and later the First World War, stimulated a broad reappraisal in the Argentine of advantages to be derived from the external connection as had the transmission of the 1873 crisis to Chile a decade and a half earlier. Short-lived cyclical fluctuations in the seven or eight years before 1914, notably in 1907-1908 and 1912, generalised the debate across the continent, just as long-term instability of specific export prices had provoked discussion in particular countries, viz the coffee valorisation project in Brazil. These discussions barely addressed the question of imperialism directly, nor were they premised upon a rejection of the external connection. The principal objective was the formulation of policies designed to maximise opportunities yielded by the prevailing international order.

Accordingly Brazilian coffee growers persuaded government to create buffer stocks so as to regulate world prices. Mexicanisation of the railway system was devised in order to structure the network more closely to domestic requirements and increase operating efficiency. Diversification of sources of foreign borrowing, particularly the placing of new issues upon the New York money market, was in some cases a reaction to perceived competition in international markets. Occasionally tariff revisions were effected in order to foster domestic industries. Autarky or a complete rupture with foreign interests was hardly considered. Was it feasible during the period? Would it have been sensible, given the high degree of international liquidity? The efficacy and the success of these measures may be questioned. And the implementation of policies does not mean that 'imperialism' did not exist or that the agents of imperial expansion were confronted and defeated by an heroic national bourgeoisie. Yet a change in Latin American attitudes towards the end of the nineteenth century does demonstrate that some groups were aware that insertion within the world economy was not costless and that specific practical problems demanded resolution. From this approach would emerge during the inter-war decades and beyond a more considered approach to the management of relations with the great powers and the world economy at large. The tenor of the debate also revealed that, by the beginning of the twentieth century, many of the republics were more complex societies than those which crystallised at the time of independence.

Perhaps imperialism and dependence is a matter of perception and definition. If, moving the discussion away from a simple question of territorial expansion, imperialism is presented as an asymmetrical relationship between systems, then for the greater part of the period studied the countries of Latin America suffered/enjoyed a colonial status. Trade with Britain or the United States was of a greater importance to individual republics than were commercial relations with that country to either North Atlantic nation. The external sector dominated the money economy or accounted for a very large share of aggregate economic activity in many republics - approximately a quarter of GDP in the Argentine by the turn of the century - but was not necessarily of greater relative significance than in Britain at the time. More sophisticated definitions of dependence refer to the shaping of a weak state in order to conform to the requirements of another, to the distortion of endogenous socio-economic structures in order to secure the interests of the metropolis. Clearly during the nineteenth century Latin America was influenced by imported ideologies and absorbed foreign capital and people as a result of which prevailing structures and institutions were modified. The critical issue is whether or not Latin America was thereby locked into an immutable relationship with external forces. Was the relationship such that, notwithstanding

changes in the form of the external connection over time, the substance
of the relationship remained exploitative and was externally perpetuated
to the detriment of Latin America? Was erratic growth, while others
developed, the unique and limited benefit conferred upon the region?
For some countries this was undoubtedly the case. External forces
sustained or created structures which inhibited dynamic change and
forged an unequal relationship with the world outside. Elsewhere,
however, a different pattern emerged – of growth with sectoral
diversification and social differentiation and the beginnings, by 1914,
of a capacity for self-sustaining expansion.

The debate about dependency and imperialism has produced a
reconsideration of the continent's external relationships. It has
compelled a focus upon internal structures and external forces and the
interaction between these agents and actors. In particular the
controversy has produced a closer examination of forms of, and shifts
in, the pattern of the external connection, yielding a differentiated
dynamic model, where hitherto uniformity was thought to prevail and a
static analysis sufficient to explain the nature of the relationship.

1. A conventional approach may be found in C.W.Arnade, A.P.Whitaker and
   B.W.Diffie, 'Causes of the Spanish American Wars of Independence',
   Journal of Inter-American Studies, II, 2, 1960, pp.125-44. For a
   synthesis of traditional and modern approaches see J.Lynch, The
   Spanish American Revolutions (London, 1973).

2. Perhaps the best recent revisionist study is J.I.Dominguez,
   Insurrection or Loyalty: the Breakdown of the Spanish American
   Empire (Cambridge, Mass., 1980). Sound national studies are
   T.E.Anna, The Fall of Royal Government in Peru (Lincoln, 1979) and
   M.Izard, El Miedo a la Revolución: La Lucha por la Libertad en
   Venezuela (Madrid, 1979). See also T.Halperin Donghi, The Aftermath
   of Revolution in Latin America (New York, 1973). Halperin, an early
   exponent of the 'Civil War' thesis, develops the theme of social
   disintegration and elite fears of profound social upheaval.

3. R.A.Humphreys, 'British Merchants and South American Independence',
   Proceedings of the British Academy, LI, 1965, pp.151-74.

4. S.J. and B.H.Stein, The Colonial Heritage of Latin America: Essays
   on Economic Dependence in Perspective (New York, 1970) pp.86-8;
   K.R.Maxwell, 'Pombal and the Nationalization of the Luso-Brazilian
   Economy', Hispanic American Historical Review (hereafter HAHR),
   XLVIII, 4, 1968, pp.608-31; Lynch, Spanish American Revolutions,
   passim. For more detailed discussion of attempts by the Marques de
   Pombal, chief minister to José I between 1755 and 1777, to modernize
   the Portuguese empire see K.R.Maxwell, Conflicts and Conspiracies:
   Brazil and Portugal 1750-1808 (Cambridge, 1973). For the impact of
   the Bourbon reforms see J.R.Fisher, Government and Society in
   Colonial Peru: the Intendant System, 1784-1814 (London, 1970) and

J.Lynch, Spanish Colonial Administration, 1782–1810: the Intendant System in the Viceroyalty of the Río de la Plata (London, 1958).

5. M.P.Costeloe, 'Spain and the Latin American Wars of Independence: the Free Trade Controversy, 1810–1820', HAHR, LXI, 2, 1981, pp.209–234; J.Fisher, '"Imperial Free Trade" and the Hispanic Economy, 1776–1796', Journal of Latin American Studies, XIII, 1, 1981, pp.21–56.

6. Lynch, Spanish American Revolutions, pp. 20–1.

7. These themes are discussed at length in P.K.Liss, Atlantic Empires: the Network of Trade and Revolution, 1713–1826 (Baltimore, 1983), see especially chapters 7 to 9.

8. The classic text is C.C.Griffin, 'Economic and Social Aspects of the Era of Spanish-American Independence', HAHR, XXIX, 2, 1949, pp.170–187.

9. A continent-wide presentation of the ECLA thesis is available in C.Furtado, Economic Development of Latin America: Historical Background and Contemporary Problems (Cambridge, 2nd edition, 1977) and O.Sunkel, O Marco Historico do Processo Desenvolvimento–– Subdesenvolvimento (Sao Paulo, 3rd edition, 1975).

10. A.G.Frank, Capitalism and Underdevelopment in Latin America: Historical Studies of Chile and Brazil (London, 1971). Frank subsequently expanded the hypothesis of a capitalist penetration of Latin America in several texts, notably in World Accumulation, 1492–1789 (London, 1978) chapter 1 especially pp.44–50.

11. Steins, op. cit., passim, especially pp.7, 9, 11, 21, 26, 101–2, 155; Frank, Capitalism and Underdevelopment pp.36, 39–40, 181, 184.

12. The outlines of free trade imperialism were first established in J.Gallagher and R.F.Robinson, 'The Imperialism of Free Trade', Economic History Review (hereafter EHR, vi, 1, 1953, pp.1–15, and subsequently in their monograph Africa and the Victorians: the Official Mind of Imperialism (London, 1961). Robinson later refined the discussion in an essay entitled, 'Non-European Foundations of European Imperialism: Sketch for a Theory of Collaboration', in R.Owen and B.Sutcliffe eds., Studies in the Theory of Imperialism (London, 1972). See also B.Semmel, The Rise of Free Trade Imperialism 1750–1850 (Cambridge, 1970) chapter 1. For differing reactions to the Gallagher and Robinson thesis by Latin Americanists see W.A.Matthew, 'The Imperialism of Free Trade: Peru 1820–70', EHR xxi, 3, 1968, pp.562–79; D.C.M.Platt, 'The Imperialism of Free Trade: some Reservations', EHR xxi, 2, 1968, pp.296–306, 'Further Objections to an "Imperialism of Free Trade", 1830–60', EHR, xxvi, 1, 1973, pp.77–91; R.Graham, 'Robinson and Gallagher in Latin America', in W.R.Louis ed., Imperialism; the Robinson Gallagher Controversy (New York, 1975); P.E.Winn, 'British Informal Empire in Uruguay in the Nineteenth Century', Past and Present, 73, 1976, pp.100–126.

13. Gallagher and Robinson, 'The Imperialism of Free Trade', loc cit, p.3.

14. This approach has recently been consolidated by authors writing from a world-system perspective. See I.Wallerstein, The Modern World System vol 1. Capitalist Agriculture and the Origins of the European World Economy in the Sixteenth Century (New York, 1974) and I.Wallerstein and T.Hopkins, 'Structural Transformations of tthe World Economy', in R.Rubenstein ed., Dynamics of World Development (Beverly Hills, 1981). Absorbing aspects of the Gallagher and Robinson hypothesis, Wallerstein's writing constitutes both a vindication of, and an advance upon, the early work of Frank. Wallerstein offers a dynamic framework centred upon interstate relations. In place of the dual model elaborated by Frank he provides a three level division of the world economy; core, semi-periphery and periphery. Wallerstein's account of the peripheral state is more comprehensive than Frank's satellite and shares some of the characteristics of Robinson's collaborative elite: both, possessing institutional cohesion, are secure against domestic opponents.

15. For Frank's response see 'Dependency is Dead: Long Live Dependency and the Class Struggle', World Development V, 4, 1977, and a revised version which appears in his book Critique and Anti-Critique: Essays on Development and Reformism (New York, 1984) chapters 24 and 25.

16. F.H.Cardoso and E.Faletto, Dependency in Latin America (London, 1979). The shorter Spanish text was published in 1969, based on a Portuguese working draft of 1967.

17. Early contributions which questioned Latin America's pattern of export-led growth are A.Encina, Nuestra Inferioridad Económica (Santiago, 1912), and A.Molina Enriquez, Los Grandes Problemas Nacionales (Mexico, 1909). More specifically focused is the work of A.E.Bunge, La Desocupación en la Argentina (Madrid, 1917), Riqueza y Renta de la Argentinna (Buenos Aires, 1917): Bunge also comments generally on sectoral and social distortions in the Argentine at the turn of the century. Works which discuss imperialism directly, and also advocate the need for fundamental institutional reform or revolution are J.Ingenieros, La Evolución de las Ideas Argentinas, 2 vols (Buenos Aires, 1918) and J.C.Mariategui, 7 Ensayos de Interpretación de la realidad Peruana (Lima, 1928).

18. For a particularly gloomy 'contemporary' view se E.Martinez Estrada, X-Ray of the Pampa (Austin, 1971, translated from the 1933 Spanish Edition). More sterident are the works of Ingenieros, La Evolución and R.Scalbrini Ortiz, El Hombre que está Solo y Espera (Buenos Aires, 1931). For a modern view see D.Denoon, Settler Capitalism: the Dynamics of Dependent Development in the Southern Hemisphere (Oxford, 1983) and S.Solberg, Immigration and Nationalism: Argentina and Chile, 1890-1914 (Austin, 1970).

19. Platt's principal contributions are set out in the Bibliographical Notes.

20. H.S.Ferns, Britain and Argentina in the Nineteenth Century (Oxford, 1960).

# Economic Penetration and the Scramble for Southern Africa

## MALYN NEWITT

### I. The Economic Causes

#### 1. Introduction

The thesis of this paper is that rapid changes in the world economy caused profound economic, social and political changes to African societies which colonial and metropolitan governments were powerless to control. They sparked off a series of local political crises which continually forced European and colonial authorities to make decisions and to adopt, often reluctantly, a 'trouble-shooting' or 'crisis management' role. In acting out this role their decisions were guided by the need to appease the dominant local interests which alone could ensure the stability necessary to safeguard the wider national interests.

During the nineteenth century, Africa experienced the force first of the commercial and then the industrial revolutions. So fast did the waves of economic change break on the continent that, in the latter part of the century, it was possible to find traditional subsistence econo̶m̶ies, slave and ivory trading networks, peasant commercial farming, plantation agriculture and industrial mining and railway complexes - all the phases of Africa's economic evolution - co-existing within the same geographical region. The decision whether or not to extend formal colonial rule was irrelevant to the development of this economic revolution. Economic and social change was proceeding almost as if the colonial frontiers had not been there. The decisions of European governments to establish formal colonies often represented the shortest of short term attempts to stabilise a fast changing balance of forces and such decisions lasted only as long as it took the next wave of economic change to break over the continent.

## 2. The Boom in the Slave Trade

Prior to the sixteenth century the muslim trading system of the Indian Ocean had barely affected southern Africa, most of which lay beyond the region of safe monsoon navigation. The Portuguese, British and Dutch, however, expanded ivory trading as far south as the Natal coast, bought foodstuffs at Table Bay and in southern Madagascar and developed a large scale export of slaves from Angola and the Congo to America. Between the sixteenth and mid-eighteenth centuries, in spite of fluctuations, there was a steady growth in the volume of this economic activity but little change in the basic network of inland fairs and trading caravans that supplied it.

In the second half of the eighteenth century, however, the rapid development of the French sugar colonies in the Indian Ocean greatly increased demand until by 1790 some 8,000 slaves were being exported each year from Mozambique. Then, early in the nineteenth century, Britain secured international agreement to the ending of the slave trade north of the equator with the result that exports from southern Africa increased dramatically. Slavers from Brazil and Cuba, which were experiencing a major revival of their sugar industries, began to appear in Mozambique ports where they competed with the French for slaves. By the 1820s, between 12,000 and 15,000 slaves were being shipped annually from the single port of Quelimane which in the eighteenth century had seldom exported 1,000.(1)

New groups became involved in the trade. In Mozambique the Macua, who had played little part in the ivory trade, took to slaving; in Madagascar the coastal chiefs embarked on their dramatic seaborne raids on Africa's coasts and islands; in Angola the increased demand led to the emergence of new networks which by-passed the old chiefly control of the trade and led to the rise of regional chiefs and headmen as principals in it. There is evidence of old ivory trading networks adapting themselves for the supply of slaves. In Zambesia the Afro-Portuguese chiefs, who for centuries had organised gold and ivory trading caravans, turned to slaving; while further south in Delagoa Bay the traditional ivory and cattle trading networks increasingly supplied slaves as well.

The boom in slaving also helped to develop new trading ports, particularly on the Indian Ocean coast, and attracted new trading capital. In eastern Africa much of this working capital derived from Indian commercial houses and in western Africa it came principally from Brazil and America. However, Portuguese and French supplied part of the new investment. Inevitably some of it also became fixed capital and fine buildings came to grace the slaving ports like Ibo, Luanda and Mozambique Island.

Finally the growth in the slave trade led to a marked increase in commercial transactions and the consumption of imports. In west Africa the steadily rising exports of slaves had principally served to stimulate the import of firearms, but in southern Africa the picture was more complex. Many of the transactions were conducted with Mexican or Spanish dollars and the variety of imports was greater. Many African chiefs began to wear European clothes and to import luxuries ranging from champagne to pianos. The habits of consumption thus acquired proved hard to get rid of and stimulated the search for other exportable commodities once the slave trade had been abolished.

3. <u>Abolition of the Slave Trade and its Effects</u>

Until the late 1840s the southern African slave trade
continued to grow in volume and to extend the impact of the world
economy to the deepest recesses of the continent. In 1842, however,
Britain obtained from Portugal a treaty allowing the arrest of ships on
suspicion of being slavers. This merely drove the trade from the major
ports to the smaller harbours and inlets but when in 1853 Brazil agreed
to ban slave imports and Cuba and the United States followed in the
1860s, the Atlantic slave trade virtually ceased to exist. There
survived only the internal trade and clandestine traffic with islands
like Sao Tomé and Madagascar.

As a result of this gradual strangling of the trade, the
economy of central Africa experienced a severe depression with all the
impoverishment, unemployment and social dislocation that accompanies a
depression in more advanced economies. In the inland areas of Angola
the old trading fairs went into decline; chiefs lost the revenue earned
from the trade and the control over guns and luxury imports. On the
coast, ships lay idle and capital was unproductive, while the old
trading networks began to disintegrate. Meanwhile large numbers of
slaves accumulated unsold in the hands of dealers who disposed of them
to chiefs and other buyers within Africa. In some cases these slaves
were recruited into armies which launched warlords on careers of
conquest and the middle years of the century saw the rise of many of
these war-bands which began by raiding their neighbours and, in some
cases, ended by forming new states in the interior. The Afro-Portuguese
chiefs of the Zambesi provide a classic case study of an elite changing
from ivory to slave trading and then responding to the contraction of
the overseas slave trade by embarking on conquests in the interior.
North of the Zambesi the sultan of Angoche also responded to abolition
by extending his political control among the coastal Macua, while
further inland slave trading chiefs like Mlozi and Jumbe established
their power on Lake Malawi and Msiri built up a formidable state in
Katanga. Angola witnessed the rise of the Cokwe warbands, armed with
guns and backed by large numbers of former slaves, whose expansion from
the 1870s led to the breaking up of the historic Lunda monarchy.

The accumulation of large numbers of slaves had economic as
well as military implications. Peoples whose economies had been largely
kin-based had to absorb increasing numbers of kinless men, or clients.
These could be employed in agriculture or in gathering forest products,
allowing for a considerable increase in exportable surpluses and a major
concentration of economic power in the hands of slave-owners. The
evolution of the Ngoni states after 1820 particularly illustrates this
trend. By their military expansion the Ngoni contributed significantly
to the flow of slaves to the coast and only the captive women and
children had been absorbed into Ngoni society. With the end of the
slave trade large numbers of male captives also accumulated in the hands
of the Ngoni kings and chiefs, thereby altering the economic and social
relations on which their states rested.(2) Another example is provided
by the Voortrekkers. By the time the Boers had established themselves
north of the Vaal in the 1840s large numbers of slaves were becoming
available in the markets to the north. The Boers were able to import
'apprentices' to meet their labour requirements. The Merina rulers of
Madagascar also accumulated large numbers of slaves and continued to

import them for the rest of the century. The slave work force allowed the Merina to divert their own manpower into the army that carried out the great expansion of their kingdom in the middle years of the century. The large amounts of capital invested in slaves also influenced the economic development of the island, the slave-owners with their estimated 50-60,000 porters dominating the transport system and thereby controlling overseas trade and the exploitation of natural resources.(3)

## 4. Expansion of 'legitimate' trade

Had no alternative commercial activity appeared to replace the slave trade, the social and political disruption of the depression would have been far more serious. However, in pressing for abolition Britain had always maintained that the high value of the slave trade destroyed other forms of commerce, and that as the slave trade declined the demand for other African products would grow. In this belief she was not alone. The civil wars in Portugal had, by the 1840s, brought to power a group of liberal politicians who wanted to destroy the foundations of absolutist, Miguelist power. Their legislation attacked the church, feudal land tenures and restrictive monopolies like the royal monopoly in ivory trading. They were anxious to see free commerce, investment and settlement replace the old economic system which had depended on slaves exported by a closed ring of dealers in league with a corrupt clique of governors and officials.

The establishment of British rule at the Cape in 1806 occurred at a time when free-trade policies were being developed throughout the British empire. New markets were opened for Cape wine and grain and their production expanded. At the same time the demand for wool by British industry led to a spectacular growth in wool production and a rapid spread of sheep farming in the Cape. The market for cattle also grew. The cattle trade at Delagoa Bay had been increasing rapidly at the end of the eighteenth century to supply visiting British and American ships and in 1817 the British governor of Mauritius negotiated a treaty with the Merina king of Madagascar allowing for an expansion of the cattle trade and the abolition of slaving. Expanding cattle exports were accompanied by the development of a leather industry organised by missionaries of the London Missionary Society. As the century advanced the demand for cattle and cattle products showed no signs of abating. Live cattle were driven to the ports and were shipped along with increasing quantities of hides and wool. In 1824 a new trading port was founded at Durban and Cape traders began to open regular commercial links with south west Africa.

Wool and cattle exports had a profound effect in the interior. The cattle-based societies of the Ngoni, Sotho and Tswana in the east and the Ovambo, Herero and Nama in the west all felt pressure on their traditional herding practices. Cattle could no longer be hoarded for use in their social and political transactions, they had become items of value in international commerce. Nor was natural increase any longer sufficient to replace cattle exchanged for guns, clothes or liquor, and raiding the herds of neighbours became a tempting alternative.(4) For a time the demand for cattle co-existed with a continuing demand for slaves, and the profits of raiding were considerable. Cattle and slaves were the rewards for the military expansion both of the Ngoni in the 1830s and 1840s and of the Ovambo in

39

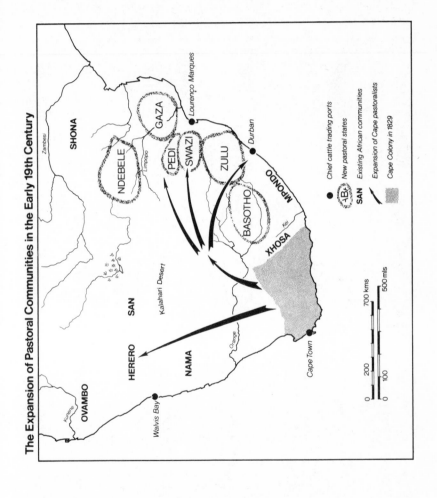

The Expansion of Pastoral Communities in the Early 19th Century

the 1880s. However the expansion of the pastoral economy also lay behind the migrations of various groups out of the narrow strip of Cape colony.

For a century the farmers of the Cape had produced their wine, tobacco and grain for the market provided by visiting ships. On the inland frontier, however, a different kind of economy had flourished. Here cattle farmers grazed their stock, hunters sent back loads of ivory and skins and traders exchanged commodities with the African communities. Early in the nineteenth century, the frontier of the Cape began to move rapidly. Armed bands of hunters and pastoralists crossed the Orange and pushed deep into Damaraland, descended the Drakensberg into Natal and crossed the Vaal and headed north onto the high veldt. These mounted warbands went under various names – Koranna, Griqua, Voortrekkers, Oorlams, Bastards – and enjoyed the technical superiority of guns, horses and wagons which enabled them to harry the scattered pastoral peoples they encountered. They skirted the high mountains of Basutoland and the densely peopled eastern Cape. After an initial clash with the Zulus they stayed clear also of the Zulu and Swazi kingdoms; they also avoided the deserts of the Kalahari and the tse-tse infested regions of the Limpopo, but they gradually established a number of new political systems in the southern interior, the counterparts of the Ngoni states to the north and east and the states formed by the former slavers in central Africa. Historians have almost exclusively studied the movements of those who called themselves Voortrekkers and have seen in them a reflection of the tensions of white society and the emergence of a form of proto-nationalism. However, the Voortrekkers, like their African and Coloured contemporaries, were responding to the increased demand for cattle, hides and wool. They needed new pastures for their expanded herds and they needed to replenish their stock by systematically raiding and expropriating the weaker peoples of the high veldt.

Closely connected with this went the expansion of the hunting economy. The abolition of the ivory trading monopoly in Angola in the 1830s led to a great increase in demand that launched the Cokwe on their militant commercial expansion, while the introduction of improved rifles greatly increased the success of the hunt. Hunters connected to one of the groups from the Cape also began to harry the game deeper into South West Africa, the Kalahari and southern Mozambique. Most of them employed professional African hunters and drew the peoples of the region deeper into the commercial network that ultimately depended on the demand for billiard balls and piano keys in the drawing rooms and clubs of Victorian England.

The expansion of hunting and pastoralism is the most obvious example of the developing world economy triggering political change in the African interior, but the expanding industrial economies provided markets for other commodities as well. Demand for various crops grown by African farmers – maize, rice, sesame, groundnuts and cashew – experienced rapid growth in demand and many African peoples took to growing for the market to replenish their depleted stocks of cattle. As surpluses were often small and unpredictable, trade came to depend on the development of an infrastructure for collection and transport, and by the second half of the century this infrastructure had been formed. Indian merchants from East Africa, many of them still involved in clandestine slaving operations, extended their commercial networks southwards into Mozambique and Madagascar, collecting and marketing sesame, cashew and groundnuts. In Angola this role was played by the funantes, or itinerant traders, and after 1880 by the Boers who trekked into the Huila highlands and who made huge profits from providing a wagon transport network.(5) Further south it was the missions which played the major role in the expansion of peasant agriculture.

Missionary societies were the product of the evangelical revival associated with the industrial revolution in England and their attitudes were deeply coloured by the economic individualism of Victorian England. Beyond the colonial frontiers of the Cape there was, by the 1840s, a strong mission presence among the Griqua, Xhosa, Sotho and Tswana. A 'second front' was opened in the 1860s, under the influence of David Livingstone, with missions established in the Lake Malawi area, Barotseland and the Congo. These missions saw it as their task to promote peasant agriculture, seeing in the thriving peasant family producing for the market, the perfect alternative to the polygamous, communal economy that sustained pagan African society. It is no coincidence that groups like the Mfengu, who had lost their chiefs and had been driven from their land, took most readily to peasant agriculture, while among the Xhosa, integration into the cash economy of the Cape was both cause and effect of the political and military disasters that overtook the traditional Xhosa chieftaincies between 1834 and 1857. Missionaries promoted the technology which alone made peasant agriculture possible - irrigation, the ox-plough and the wagon - and they provided markets where produce could be sold and exchanged. They also preached the work ethic which, it is sometimes alleged, was the ideal preparation for the ultimate destiny of their converts as wage labourers within the white economy. In some cases the missions had direct commercial links with Europe, striking examples being the African Lakes Company which came into existence in 1877 as the commercial arm of the Scottish missions around Lake Malawi and the marriage alliance between the head of the Methodist mission in Pondoland and the leading European trader in the region.(6)

This expansion of peasant production had nothing to do with formal colonial rule. It took place alike inside and outside the colonial borders, among the pacified Xhosa of the Ciskei and among the still independent Xhosa of the Transkei. It took place in areas of Mozambique nominally under Portuguese rule and in areas still outside. In Madagascar it took place in a community still wholly free from colonial control. Wherever it occurred, however, it had the effect of sapping the foundations of traditional, communal societies in which the fertility of land, cattle and women was closely controlled by the chief. Chiefs were themselves drawn into this process. Surplus slaves were put to work in the fields and the surplus cattle acquired on raids were traded to the eager agents of the export companies. The desire to buy guns provided a powerful incentive to enter the market economy.

Expanding world trade provided markets for products that could be gathered in the forests as well as those that could be grown. Wax, honey and wild gums had always been lucrative exports and their volume could only be expanded by ever deeper penetration into the interior. Wild rubber, in particular, grew throughout central Africa and in the 1870s world demand created a boom of sensational proportions. Peoples throughout the interior began to collect the latex and caravans

were organised to move large quantitites to the coast. Prominent among
those who organised trading caravans were the Cokwe, the Ovimbundu and,
in Mozambique, the Makonde. This increase in foreign trade brought new
wealth and power to the caravan leaders who were able to compete with
traditional chiefs for the control of firearms. Many of them usurped
chiefly power or forced the chiefs also into the field of international
trading in order to survive. To a greater extent even than the trade in
grain and cattle, rubber brought the peoples of central Africa into the
world economy. Exceptionally high prices persuaded peoples remote in
the interior to adapt their economies to the production and transport of
rubber. When demand eventually fell away in the 1910s those who, for a
generation, had depended on the trade were to be ruined.(7)

## 5. Plantation Capital

Before the nineteenth century the use of capital to finance
production in Africa had been confined to the French investments in the
plantations of the Mascarene and Seychelles islands. Then, in the early
years of the nineteenth century, the Arabs of Zanzibar began to grow
cloves on slave-run plantations in east Africa and the French sugar
interests from Réunion (and to a lesser extent the British from
Mauritius) began to look for new areas suitable for production. The
islands off the coast of Madagascar had virgin soil and a suitable
climate, transport was easy and it was thought there would be convenient
access to supplies of cheap labour. In 1821 the French had occupied
Sainte Marie and in 1842 Nossi Bé and Mayotte. By 1850, with world
sugar prices rapidly rising, the planters had begun to strip the forest
cover for plantations. In the late 1840s the enterprise of William
Sunley also brought sugar to Anjouan and the 1850s saw extensive
investment in sugar plantations in Natal.

In western Africa, the development of plantation agriculture
was slower to get established, but local Portuguese governors began to
experiment with the production of tropical products as part of a move to
break the old slave trading rings. Land was made available in the
Cazengo highlands of Angola for the production of coffee and in spite of
early set-backs the wave of rising prices soon led to coffee production
becoming firmly established. Much of the capital invested came from the
profits of local trade. Similar investments were being made in Sao Tomé
and in the 1850s the first sugar planters began to clear land in the
coastal oases of southern Angola, their sugar being used to provide rum
for inland trade.(8)

Plantation agriculture was, of course, as labour-intensive in
Africa as it had been in America, yet it had to establish itself at a
time when the slave trade was under attack. The French islands felt the
problem most acutely and switched to a system of engagé labour which
during the 1850s merely perpetuated slavery under another name. This
was only ended when Britain allowed the import of Indian contract labour
into Réunion as well as Mauritius in the 1860s. Even so, the French
continued to make use of Arab-owned slaves in the Comoro Islands, a
device which Sunley also used and which lost him his appointment as
British Consul in Anjouan.

In Natal, plantations were at first supplied with slaves
'freed' by British cruisers but when these failed to provide enough

labour and when local Africans refused to work in the plantations, contract workers and then Indians were imported – the first of the Indians arriving in 1860. In the 1870s plantation agriculture spread to the lower Zambesi, an area whose soil and climate were ideally suited to it. The delta region had by this time become sufficiently pacified for a number of concessionnaires to begin the cultivation of sugar and opium. Opium proved a failure but the Zambesi sugar industry grew and further plantations were opened at different points along the coast. Until 1875 slavery remained legal in Mozambique and Angola and was widely employed. When it was banned, the pressure of local economic interests ensured that it was replaced by a system of enforced contract labour which kept the plantations supplied.

To be successful, plantations required an economic infrastructure and government support. Transport was important, though not a major problem for those in coastal areas; security for crops and for fixed assets was essential; and government aid was required for the provision and retention of a labour force. Although plantation owners were initially able to export their produce on a rising world market, they began to look to colonial governments to stimulate local consumption when prices became unstable in the 1880s.

What might loosely be described as plantation capital penetrated regions beyond the formal colonial frontiers, often with bizarre and unpredictable results. By the 1860s the 'concession racket' was well established, as the example of Egypt showed. European financiers and entrepreneurs negotiated concessions to supply money, goods or services to rulers with clauses attached that either proved ruinous to the states concerned or allowed compensation to be claimed for default. The French proved particularly adept at exploiting these opportunities and extended the system to the Indian Ocean.

Rulers most vulnerable to these adventurers were those anxious to acquire the material benefits of western civilisation. The Merina rulers of Madagascar had expanded their power partly through their close association with the British in Mauritius who had supplied the military hardware for their conquests. The penetration of European traders and missionaries which followed gave rise to deep factional splits within the Merina ruling class and the temporary triumph in 1835 of elements hostile to christianity and to Europe. The habits of consumption among the Merina aristocracy had, however, already been established and the conflicting desires to prevent the entry of Europeans into the country while permitting the flow of consumer goods proved a seed-bed unusually fertile for the individual entrepreneur who could negotiate monopolies in close association with one of the dominant factions. Jean Laborde was the first such monopolist contracting with the Madagascar rulers to introduce a wide range of European technologies. However, Laborde, for all his influence, never dominated the powerful figure of queen Ranavalona. Jean François Lambert was different. Gaining the support of the heir to the throne, Lambert secured a 'charter' granting him extensive lands, mineral rights and privileges which were recognised in a treaty when Radama came to the throne in 1862. To prevent this domination of their country, the Malagasy lords murdered Radama and freed themselves from Lambert's 'charter' by the payment of a massive indemnity to France.

Lambert himself moved on to obtain a similar concession from the female ruler of the tiny island of Mohéli in 1869. By the terms of this charter, Lambert acquired the right to exploit any land he chose in Mohéli and was to have the labour to do it. A similar concession was obtained by the naturalist, Léon Humblot, to exploit the island of Grande Comore – a concession which established Humblot as effective master of the island and the population as his serfs.

The rulers who signed these contracts may well have been ignorant but they were not entirely naive. The contracts appeared greatly to strengthen the ruler's position vis à vis rival factions; they assured him some element of control over the introduction of western goods and technologies which the free trade treaties pressed for earlier in the century by British and French did not. It was a characteristic of the concessions of Lambert and Humblot that the rulers were made a party to a business contract, at one stroke changing their position as sovereign into one of principal shareholder in an enterprise. The long term implications were not, at first, apparent and in the short term such a change was attractive to make.(9)

The activities of these French entrepreneurs, as of their German, British and Portuguese counterparts elsewhere in Africa, was not the sign of a vigorous and expanding capitalism – indeed it was the tactics of those with weak financial backing. Britain's powerful trading position had led her to favour freedom of trade. France, however, could not compete commercially and the major French financial institutions were not prepared, in the 1860s and 1870s, for speculative ventures. French interests in the Indian Ocean therefore, resorted to this form of disguised brigandage in which local rulers were hoodwinked into using their authority to divert the revenues and resources of their states into French hands.

6. The Mining Revolution

Although, by the 1860s southern Africa had been profoundly influenced by expanding world trade, it remained of only peripheral interest to European and American economies. Wool, sugar, coffee and cattle were all commodities which could be obtained elsewhere and their production in Africa was largely due to certain favourable marginal factors like virgin land, cheap labour and the unique conditions of the early years of the century which allowed the pastoral economies to expand through the large scale expropriation of the land and stock of others. However, the relative unimportance of southern Africa to the world economy was best seen in the reluctance of white emigrants to settle and in the failure of railway investment, in contrast to the massive influx of people and funds into the United States. In the late 1860s, however, all this was to change.

One by-product of the movement of the ivory hunting frontier deeper into Africa had been the amateur exploration and prospecting undertaken by the hunters. In the 1860s some of these began to report gold north of the Orange and mines were opened at Lydenburg and Tati although transport over hundreds of miles of veldt had to be made by the painfully slow ox-wagon. In 1867 the first alluvial diamonds were found and by 1870 the world's richest diamond mines had been opened at Kimberley on the fringes of the Kalahari. The mines at once attracted

capital investment and immigration on a scale previously unknown in
Africa and accompanying these developments came a host of social and
political problems all requiring government initiatives. Not only were
gold and diamonds found hundred of miles in the interior but they were
in areas where political authority was of the most shadowy kind. To
exploit the mines, railways had to be built, security provided, a
legislative structure for the development of the industry drawn up and
matters of public health and the organisation of food supplies and
labour demanded attention. As capital flowed into southern Africa, the
railways advanced and mining operations expanded, new towns grew up and
the demand for food – and hence land values – soared. A whole range of
ancillary services and industries came into existence. The young Cecil
Rhodes, for example, made his first money providing pumping equipment to
the mines.

Railways were, in time, to transform the economy of the
African interior, but the most immediate impact of the mining revolution
was felt in the demand for labour. The diamond mines came to employ
30,000 black workers and the railway contractors as many more, all of
whom had to be brought in from long distances. At first the search for
labour was so desperate that the Kimberley authorities allowed the sale
of firearms as an attraction. This policy naturally caused extreme
opposition among whites and systematic labour recruitment began to be
organised. Labour touts travelled in the interior persuading chiefs to
'encourage' their men to volunteer. How much 'encouragement' was needed
is arguable, for African society was already so conditioned by earlier
commercial contacts that mine wages and the possibility of buying guns
were sufficient incentive for volunteers to come forward. Whatever the
cause, by the mid-1870s the great migration of black workers had begun
and one of the fundamental characteristics of modern South African life
was established. It was only intensified when further gold discoveries
were made on the Witwatersrand and in Rhodesia in the 1880s and 1890s.

## 7. Ecology, Drought and Migrant Labour

Mines and plantations affected the African population
principally through their incessant demands for labour. These demands
were first raised at a time when unsold slaves were accumulating in the
hands of chiefs and dealers, and in some cases this led to slaves,
originally bound for export, being utilised in local production. In
eastern Africa this happened in Zanzibar, Madagascar and the Comoro
Islands, while in western Africa this was the source of labour for the
planters of Sao Tomé and Angola. Elsewhere the link between the slave
trade and labour supply was more indirect. Unsold slaves were employed
by chiefs in agriculture, hunting and herding, releasing the young males
of the clan for migrant labour.

Migrant labour in southern Africa began early in the century
when Xhosa on the eastern frontier entered the Cape for seasonal work,
taking back with them guns, horses and cattle. One by one other
population groups, suffering from Zulu raids or losses of land and
cattle, turned to wage labour within the white economy to seek survival.
For the most part chiefs encouraged this departure of migrant workers.
The need to make good losses of cattle and to acquire wagons and horses
overcame any reluctance they may have had at seeing their control over
production and consumption within their society impaired. Moreover,

improvements in firearms technology forced chiefs to replace antique muzzle-loaders with modern breach-loading rifles. Migrant labour soon acquired a momentum of its own. Bride price in southern Mozambique came increasingly to be paid in gold sterling rather then in the traditional cattle, while the taste for European consumer goods both among chiefs and ordinary people turned these into necessities of life.

It is ecological factors, however, that do most to explain the rapid break down of traditional African economies and their growing dependence on the colonial sector. Central and southern Africa suffers periodically from drought, and droughts usually span a number of years. To survive at all, most African peoples have had to be mobile, and migration and shifting cultivation form a common thread in their stories. Even shifting cultivation, however, could not always save the delicately balanced ecology in times of drought, and famine and starvation resulted. Drought caused mortality rates to rise and the inhabitants of marginal land were forced into better watered areas, raiding their neighbours for cattle and food. Drought was one of the major factors which fed the central African slave trade with victims – the surge in exports from Angola in the 1780s and Zambesia in the 1820s coming at a time of severe drought. Drought was usually followed by locusts and the outbreak of disease which attained epidemic proportions among human and animal populations weakened by malnutrition. Repeatedly in the nineteenth century African populations were struck by crippling epidemics of smallpox and typhoid, while cattle herds were decimated with red-water fever and rinderpest.

It is now clear that drought and ecological disaster reacted with market forces and the penetration of plantation and mining capital to speed up the process of absorption into the colonial economy. First, the spread of commercial peasant farming led to the intensive cultivation of land replacing traditional shifting agriculture, with the result that soils were quickly exhausted and the next drought brought disaster. Second, the advance of the hunting (ivory) and gathering (wax, honey, gum, rubber) frontier led to widespread destruction of natural resources and to the shooting out of game which had been one of the resources on which populations had been able to depend in time of drought.(10) Third, the burgeoning industrial economy was making its own depredations into the ecology of southern Africa. Wagon traffic along the fringes of the Kalahari destroyed the grasslands; wood-burning railway engines consumed the forest for miles alongside the tracks; mining towns devoured wood, water and food from huge areas around them and the desiccation of marginal lands grew steadily worse. The fact that the years 1887-1895 experienced exceptionally good rainfall merely permitted a still more intensive exploitation of these resources than would otherwise have been possible, and made the onset of drought when it occurred in 1896 still more disastrous. This time drought was accompanied by the great rinderpest outbreak which devastated cattle herds and put the finishing touches to the destruction of African independence.(11)

Drought and the destruction of the environment drove people onto the labour market. Not surprisingly migrant labour appeared preferable to death from starvation or the hazards of war and migration. The drying up of marginal land thus broke many people to the habit of working for wages. For example, the Pedi of the Transvaal and the

Tsonga of southern Mozambique who lived on marginal land, were in this way enabled to survive drought and maintain relatively high population densities. These numbers imposed still greater pressures on the land and contributed, along with commercial farming and intensified hunting, to a rapid deterioration of fertility, driving yet more people to become migrant labourers. This cycle of increasing population, increasing rural poverty and increasing dependancy thus acquired a grim inevitability. Migrant labour became one of the principal characteristics of the white economy in southern Africa. It represented a massive subsidy for employers, enabling white enterprise to reduce its labour costs below subsistence. It proved the vehicle for extending the impact of the fluctuating world economy far beyond the colonial frontiers, creating the beginnings of the regional economy which, in southern Africa, has always proved so powerful a factor overriding the colonial frontier divisions.

## II. The Political Consequences

### 8. Indirect Rule

At the end of the Napoleonic Wars, Britain, France and Portugal each maintained a formal presence in southern Africa: Britain at the Cape and Mauritius, Portugal at Luanda and Mozambique Island, and France in Réunion. In 1839 Britain established a base at Aden to act as a coaling station for the steamers between India and the Red Sea and in 1842 France established what she hoped would become a naval base at Mayotte. Although each country had its enthusiastic empire builders, especially among military and naval personnel, politics in Europe was dominated by liberal political and economic ideas. These were clearly on the ascendant in Britain in spite of the Tory dominance in politics after 1815. In Portugal and France acceptance of these ideas had to await the liberal victories of the 1830s. Liberal statesmen wanted to see an expansion of legitimate economic activity and to liberalise trade and labour relations.

Throughout the century an intricate pattern was woven between the interests of the mother countries and the local interests of dominant groups in the colonies. If the two sets of interests proved incompatible, as happened when Portugal attempted to suppress the slave trade at a time when the Afro-Portuguese trading community was still wholly dependent on it, or when Britain attempted to impose fixed frontiers on the semi-nomadic pastoral farmers of the Cape, then anarchy could result, with expensive consequences for the mother country. Ultimately the only satisfactory way of safeguarding vital national interests lay in collaborating with dominant local groups. These crude political realities forced the home governments again and again into courses of action which were defended publicly with lofty imperial raison d'état but which were in reality tailored to suit the economic interests of the collaborating groups in Africa.

Portuguese economic interests lay in the trade which came to the coasts of Angola and Mozambique from the inland fairs and Afro-Portuguese trading settlements. It was official policy to protect these by granting commissions to backwoodsmen or African chiefs to act on Portugal's behalf. These surrogates for Portuguese authority were granted the title of capitao-mor, receiving Portuguese uniforms and the right to fly the flag. They also had access to government supplies of firearms. It was a system that had to survive in a period when large Ngoni armies were invading eastern Africa and when the dislocation caused by the ending of the slave trade was promoting internal conflict, frequently between the very persons who had been given the Portuguese commissions.

In the Indian Ocean region France and Britain also to upheld their economic interests largely by indirect means. The British formed close alliances with the Omani sultans of Zanzibar and with the Merina rulers of Madagascar. In 1848 they extended their protection to the minuscule sultanate of Anjouan. The French competed with Britain for influence in Zanzibar and supported the Sakalava in Madagascar. Their principal success, however, was in Egypt where in the 1860s French interests received the commission to build the Suez Canal in the face of determined British opposition to the whole idea. This Anglo-French rivalry involved no extension of colonial territory beyond the French annexation of a few islands off Madagascar where their sugar planters became active. Both countries continued to believe that their commerce and investments could best be protected by finding friendly local regimes through which to work.

Further south, at the Cape, Britain had inherited the settlements of the Dutch East India Company and it became her policy to rule in collaboration with the dominant local interests. Close cooperation was achieved with the landowners of the western Cape who benefited greatly from the opening of British markets to their produce and who, in turn, supplied many of the judges, administrators and soldiers for the Cape government. It was less easy, however, to find a way of controlling the frontier. Various solutions were sought, all of them based on the search for some group powerful enough for the British to make the centrepiece of a policy of indirect rule. The earliest attempts at a frontier policy involved fixing boundary lines which settlers were not to cross, establishing depopulated zones, military posts and even military fairs at which trading activity was to be concentrated. Such frontier policies showed a total ignorance of the nature of a pastoral and hunting economy that was experiencing rapid growth in the demand for its products. It ignored the seasonal nature of the grazing, the needs of Cape and Xhosa pastoralists to move in search of water and new land. It ignored the interdependence of black, white and coloured in trade, herding, war and marriage. Above all it ignored the fact that semi-nomadic pastoralists can never be made amenable to central control. Pressures caused by an expanding pastoral economy artificially restricted by frontier policies devised in Cape Town built up until in the 1820s armed bands of hunters and stockmen began to leave the Cape. These rapidly established political space for themselves in an interior already devastated by war and sparsely populated.(12)

These migrations, or treks, presented the British authorities with a major dilemma. Imperial interests demanded primarily the security of the Cape sea route and the continuation of effective measures against the slave trade. They also demanded that the government of South Africa should cost as little as possible. One option was to ignore what was happening to the north, but this proved unacceptable partly because missionaries established on the frontier were able to embarrass the government through pressure groups active in Britain, and partly because the disorders associated with the treks threatened the security of the settled areas of the Cape. When the Boer trekkers in Natal raided the Pondo or the Free Staters raided the Sotho, the repercussions were felt in the Cape and troops had to be expensively deployed on the frontier.

Initially it was hoped to form a <u>cordon sanitaire</u> of protected, but not directly ruled, chieftaincies, and missionaries were given the task of maintaining these alliances in working order. Treaties were made with Griqua, Sotho and Xhosa chiefs and missionary influence expanded impressively in the transfrontier regions. Such policies were not, of course, economically neutral. The missionaries favoured specific social and economic institutions and the influence accorded to them hastened the change from communal agriculture controlled by clan heads to peasant farming by monogamous christian family units, growing for the market and looking to the missions for leadership. Such changes were slow to take place but they led to a 'colonial' transformation of African society beyond the frontiers of formal colonial rule.

A policy of protectorates proved effective only in the immediate frontier area. Beyond that the Cape authorities were under pressure to act more directly. Contacts were maintained between the Cape settlers and the trekkers, involving trade, the export of firearms and the passing of escaped criminals. Demands were heard for the protection of legitimate British interests in the interior and for the defense of established commerce at Durban. These small-scale interests, which counted for next to nothing when weighed in the balance with the rest of Britain's overseas trade and investment, were nevertheless powerful locally and were able to touch a sensitive imperial nerve by stressing the (wholly fictitious) risk of foreign intervention in southern Africa. These local interests coloured the advice which officials sent to Whitehall. In particular they influenced the decision to annex the most sensitive of the frontier areas. In 1842 troops were sent to annex Natal, in 1847 it was decided to take over the land between the Kei and Keiskamma (Ciskei) and in 1848 that between the Orange and the Vaal.

It was hoped that these annexations would stabilise the frontier and that they could be maintained cheaply with the collaboration of powerful groups whose interests had been served by annexation. These hopes were only partially realised. In the Orange River Sovereignty Britain became involved in the seemingly inextricable conflicts of Boer and Sotho farmers in the fertile Caledon valley. The thankless and, as it proved, expensive task of ruling this region was also found to be unnecessary. As long as Britain controlled the ports, she would control the trade and the flow of guns to the settlers in the interior and this seemed a more satisfactory way for Britain to conduct her relations with the landlocked Boer republics until the 1870s. The Orange River Sovereignty was, therefore, abandoned in 1854 but the other annexations were retained. Possession of Natal secured for Cape interests control of the trade of Zululand and the settlements on the high veldt. Moreover the influx of plantation capital and the large investments made by land companies soon established further powerful reasons of state for retaining Natal. The Ciskei was also retained – at first as a separate colony called British Kaffraria.

Both new colonies brought Britain the problem of ruling large African populations. The Natal government adopted Theophilus Shepstone's policy of re-establishing communal economic and social structures in large reserves. Missionaries were active but the system, designed for administrative simplicity and cheapness, failed to meet the economic objectives of the settlers who continued to demand access to African markets and to cheap labour. In the Ciskei the viability of the old communal economy was deliberately destroyed and, following the catastrophe of the cattle killings in 1857, the African population was dispersed in scattered units where they could be influenced by the missions and forced to enter the labour market and where a few could grow food surpluses for the Cape market. A policy ostensibly designed to free the imperial government from the expense of frontier wars in fact played the tune of the leading Cape economic interests and aided the expansion of the labour supply and of commercial agriculture in the eastern Cape.

## 9. The Portuguese

Having agreed at the time of their triumph in the mid-1830s to a formal ban of the slave trade, the liberal politicians in Portugal were, thereafter, placed under considerable pressure to enforce the abolition. This proved a delicate task, as everyone in the colonies, from the governor to the humblest trader, was deeply involved in the trade. Decrees from Lisbon had virtually no effect and it was realised that more effective government would be required in the interior, and that opportunities would have to be created for alternative forms of economic activity. New sources of government revenue would also have to be found once the profits of the slave trade dried up. All this pointed towards the adoption of a forward policy to consolidate colonial rule in areas where informal influence had previously been wielded only through slaving networks.

In Angola the government moved to establish garrisons in the Cazengo and Ovimbundu highlands, to collect tax from the African populations and to encourage coffee planting with grants of land. Efforts were also made to open up the Huila highlands in the south and to encourage the immigration of Portuguese and Madeirans. Infrastructure was to be improved by steamers plying on the Cuanza. The success of this policy was mixed. Attempts to collect tax from the Bakongo and the Mbundu led to widespread resistance which was also an expression of the resentment at the abolition of the slave trade. On the other hand, investment and settlement in Cazengo and Huila got fitfully under way and two new areas of European economic activity were established with expensive, if not always very effective, government backing.

In Mozambique the forward policy was forced on the Portuguese by the continuation of slaving in Zambesia and by the invasion of the area by the Gaza Ngoni who laid the trading settlements under tribute. The Portuguese wanted to end the feudal tenures which formed the basis of the power of the slave trading chiefs, to collect taxation and to encourage legitimate commerce. However, they were faced by formidable combinations among local slavers determined to resist any encroachments on their predatory way of life. In 1858 Livingstone led an expedition to the Zambesi and in 1861 missions inspired by his writings was established. Both were vocal advocates of opening the region freely to trade and made no secret of their commercial and industrial objectives. These were allies more capable of embarrassing the Portuguese than of helping them and they succeeded in pushing Portugal into adopting rash military measures in an attempt to curb the power of the slavers. In the 1860s four expeditions were sent against the main slaving strongholds, and the Portuguese suffered a series of military humiliations.(13)

## 10. South Africa in the 1870s

During the 1870s Britain once more began a policy of conquest and annexation in southern Africa and at the same time entered into negotiations with Portugal for a settlement which would have partitioned the sub-continent into spheres of influence. The principal events of the period from 1868 to 1882 include the annexation of Basutoland (1868) and its transference to the Cape in 1871; the assumption by Britain of control of Griqualand in 1871 after it had been decided that the diamond fields lay in that area; the first moves by Lord Carnarvon in 1874 to set up a confederation; the annexation of the Transvaal in 1877 and the wars against the Pedi and the Zulu between 1877 and 1879; the beginnings in 1875 of Anglo-Portuguese negotiations over tariffs, railways and other matters following the McMahon arbitration which had declared Delagoa Bay to be Portuguese. All these initiatives broke down in the early 1880s. The annexations led to widespread rebellion and to massively costly wars which spread from Transkei and Griqualand to Basutoland and eventually to the Transvaal itself. The Portuguese negotiations meanwhile ran into increasing opposition and eventually had to be abandoned, being superceded by the settlement reached by the powers at Berlin early in 1885. These bewildering events can, however, only be understood by looking at the economic changes which were forcing the hand of British and Portuguese policy makers and compelling them to adopt a wider role and a more forceful colonial policy.

The British policy of controlling the coasts and exerting indirect influence in the interior began to break down in 1868 when the Transvaalers concluded a free trade treaty with the Portuguese and opened a road to Lourenço Marques. Lourenço Marques had been the port to which African pastoralists of the interior had brought their cattle and ivory, but initial Boer attempts to use it had foundered with the failure of Trichardt's trek in 1838. Now the expanding economy of the high veldt demanded better communications and a road to Lourenço Marques offered the Boers not only the shortest route to the coast but one free from British control. At the same time the disorders accompanying pastoral expansion in south west Africa were threatening the informal hegemony of Cape commercial interests there as well.

A sober assessment of imperial interests by home governments suggested that such small commercial dealings could well be ignored, but in both regions the predatory habits of the dominant pastoral groups were leading to continuous anarchy which missionaries and traders publicised to the acute embarrassment of the government. There existed vestigial British claims to Lourenço Marques and in 1872 Britain agreed to accept the arbitration of the president of France, Marshall McMahon. When this was delivered in Portugal's favour in 1875, the possibility of a major commercial route developing outside British control had become a reality.   At the same time the Cape despatched a commissioner to arbitrate between the warring groups in south west Africa.   In this he was not particularly successful but he did persuade the Cape to take over the main trading port in Walvis Bay bringing the south west African trading system once again under Cape control.   The trade of Lourenço Marques and Walvis Bay was immeasurably small as a percentage of total British trade, but it was important to the Cape and safeguarding it helped to buy the goodwill of Cape politicians on whom Britain depended (more than ever after the Cape received responsible government in 1872) for the government of the region.   It was a tortuous chain of political logic but one which gave great significance to the commercial interests of petty coastal traders in remote parts of the world.

While Britain was trying to repair the leaking dykes of her informal empire in southern Africa, a major breach had occurred in the interior with the discovery of diamonds in territory disputed between the two Boer republics and the Griquas.   Arbitration in 1871 awarded the land to the Griqua chief, Waterboer, but it was clear that this would not lead to any permanent settlement.   Britain hoped the Cape government would assume responsibility, and annexed Griqualand in readiness to hand it over, but the Cape authorities, having recently accepted reluctant responsibility for Basutoland and British Kaffraria, refused.   Britain was, therefore, left with a minuscule, landlocked crown colony and a great deal of illwill from all the other white communities in southern Africa.

Initially Britain hoped to be able to get away with establishing in the diamond fields a vestigial administration which would pay for itself, but local circumstances decided otherwise.   The diggers demanded security, public services and labour.   Moreover, decisions had to be reached about the legal framework for exploiting claims.   The diamond mines attracted migrant workers from as far away as the Zambesi and returning miners were soon taking guns with them through Boer territory.   Firearms accumulating in African hands led to two major incidents, in Natal in 1873 and in Basutoland in 1880-1, both of which forced the imperial government to intervene and resume direct control. Eventually, with the onset of drought in 1876, Britain had to face a rebellion in Griqualand itself.   These problems forced a whole reassessment of the position of the diamond fields.   In 1876 the claims of the Free State were settled and the whole administration of the colony was reorganised in the interests of the dominant groups among the miners.   Mining law was changed to facilitate the amalgamation of claims and labour laws were introduced to control the sale of guns, to license labour contractors and to secure a controlled compound system for workers.   Kimberley was transferred in an orderly manner to the administration of the self-governing Cape in 1878 and by 1882 the diamond fields had passed into the control of one of the most enduring international monopolies, the De Beers corporation.

Already in 1874 Lord Carnarvon, the colonial secretary, had launched his attempt to create a confederation between the four white states of southern Africa.   The ostensible reason for this policy was to enable Britain to withdraw from direct involvement in southern African affairs while still securing her economic predominance and vital strategic interests. However, a solution which so neatly fitted the political facts as Britain saw them did not fit the economic facts of southern Africa. In the first place, Cape Colony, which had been unwilling to assume responsibility for the disorderly diamond fields in 1871, was still more averse to forming a federation with the equally chaotic Transvaal and Natal. The commercial interests of the Cape were best served by the old British policy of control over the seaports and access to the interior. Moreover, the Cape could, for the most part, supply its labour needs from its dependent or semi-dependent African territories of Ciskei, Transkei and Basutoland.

The Free State retained grievances against Britain over the ownership of the diamond fields, the sale of arms to migrant labourers and the sovereignty of Basutoland but, although these were all economic in origin, they were capable of political solution without the Free State being drawn into a federation. It was in Natal and the Transvaal that local economic interests precipitated Britain into disastrous political and military action. The Transvaal government had been trying to improve its route to Lourenço Marques by raising money for a railway. By 1876 these attempts had failed and it was realised that no further progress would be made without British backing. At the same time, the Transvaal became involved in war with the Pedi. The old hunting and slaving economy which had prospered in the Zoutpansberg in the 1850s and 1860s was now failing and the Boer settlements were being abandoned. The failure of the commandos against the Pedi and the fact that guns were reaching them from the mines created strong demands for British action.(14) At the same time Cape banks and land companies, whose investments were endangered by the visible failure and imminent bankruptcy of the Transvaal government also demanded British intervention. These economic pressure groups persuaded Carnarvon that there would be widespread support for a take over and in 1877 Shepstone, at the head of thirty troopers, took possession of the Transvaal for Britain.

Natal economic interests also pressed for intervention. The labour demands of the sugar planters had been met by Indian contract labour but other settlers continued to complain of a shortage and blamed Shepstone's 'native reserves' for preventing the economic advance of the colony. The continued existence of viable African subsistence economies in Natal itself, in Pondoland to the south and in Zululand to the north was hindering Natal's economic growth. In addition there was pressure to free the flow of African labour from these areas to the mines. This settler agitation was aided by missionaries and military men, and the British Transvaal authorities, anxious to appease Boer land hunger in the cheapest way, also added their weight in support of the idea that the destruction of Zulu independence was the key to a general resolution of the problems of southern Africa.(15)

Yet none of this might have been enough to trigger the disastrous Zulu War had it not been for the economic crisis produced by the cycle of drought which began to affect southern Africa seriously in 1869 and its affects ravaged the pastoral economies of Boer, Coloured and African alike. Water resources and pasture dwindled and, as so often in similar circumstances, the pastoral societies were pushed into violent conflict to escape from a crisis they could not control. Boer farmers began to press on the pastures of Zulu, Pedi and Griqua; Xhosa herdsmen raided Mfengu in Cape Colony and discontent spread into Basutoland as well. Full scale war occurred in the eastern Cape in 1877 and in Griqualand the following year. As these were beyond the capacities of the Cape government to deal with, imperial troops had to be employed. British troops were also sent to crush the Pedi. It was easy for various interested parties to suggest that it was the independence of the Zulus which was sustaining African opposition and which was the underlying cause of the general strife. Early in 1879 the decision was made to launch a rapid invasion of Zululand and on January 23rd the British army was overwhelmed and massacred by the Zulus at Isandhlwana, turning in one disastrous day a limited frontier war into a major challenge to the British empire.

The motives behind the British annexations of Basutoland, Griqualand, the Transvaal and Zululand all stemmed logically from the political plans of the Colonial Office to devolve responsibility and to withdraw from direct involvement in southern Africa. Looking back from the end of the decade, however, what had happened assumed a devastating clarity. The major independent African states south of the Limpopo had been crushed, not by the inexorable advance of white settler power, but by the direct intervention of imperial forces. The end of the political independence of the Xhosa, Pedi and Zulu had also seen the end of their independent, communal economic systems. Commercial penetration now pushed ahead, land expropriation speeded up and tens of thousands of Africans were forced onto the labour market to swell the bands of migrant workers building railways and working the mines. British policy may have been intended in Westminster to serve well defined imperial objectives; but on the spot it served the economic interests of the dominant settler groups and satisfied their demand for more land, more labour, for better communications and for the commercial penetration of African society.

## 11. The Anglo-Portuguese Treaties

In spite of the disasters delivered to Portugal by the forward colonial policy of the 1850s and 1860s, her interest in Africa continued to grow. Portugal's was a classic underdeveloped economy, selling wine and a few raw materials to Britain and receiving what capital investment came her way from British sources. The only escape from this economic dependency appeared to lie in Africa, which offered the hope of new markets for Portuguese produce and, with its great asset of cheap labour, would enable Portugal to develop plantation agriculture. Other countries might see Africa as an outlet for surplus capital, Portugal saw it as a way of generating capital for investment at home. It is significant that many people in France, after the disasters of the Franco-Prussian War, also began to view Africa as the key to future recovery and it is probable that the 'Geographical Movement' in France influenced the founding in 1875 of the Lisbon Geographical Society which became the chief agent of imperialist propaganda. The late nineteenth century saw rapid expansion in Portuguese textile production with a consequent revival of interest in potential African markets. The idea of an expanding African empire was, therefore, of increasing interest to the industrialists and wine-growers of northern Portugal. It was still little more than propaganda on the pages of the journals, however, when in 1877 Britain and Portugal began their negotiations for a bilateral treaty.

Britain's interest in Portugal's trading colonies had been growing since the 1840s. British missions had established themselves in the Zambesi and Congo areas and their humanitarian agitation was closely linked with commercial interests. In the Congo estuary the export of palm oil was becoming profitable and on the Zambesi the African Lakes Company was trying to open a steamer service for the first time. These trading interests pressed for consular protection but also agitated against the high tariffs with which Portugal had traditionally tried to protect her colonial trade. Free trade, security and improved transport formed a policy package which even the most dedicated anti-imperial free trader could espouse. To these commercial demands were added Britain's concern about Boer access to the port of Lourenço Marques. At first Britain had tried to put obstacles in the way of a railway but once the Transvaal had been annexed in 1877, building the railway became part of Britain's plan for the integration of the Transvaal into the proposed South African confederation.

The British ambassador in Lisbon and the Portuguese foreign minister, Andrade Corvo, saw the possibility of a treaty package which would serve the political and economic interests of all parties. Britain would recognise Portuguese sovereignty in the Congo estuary, and by implication, in the Congo basin as a whole, and would secure the loans necessary for the construction of the Lourenço Marques railway, and in return Portugal would lower her tariffs and allow freedom for British trade within her sphere of influence. The first treaty on these lines was drawn up in 1877 and the second, the Congo treaty, in 1882. It is clear that, if they had been accepted, they would have led to a partition of the whole of Africa south of the Congo-Zambesi watershed into British and Portuguese spheres of roughly equal sizes. These would not have been formal colonies so much as regions of economic enterprise, with each nation allowing privileged access to the other. Trade would be free, communications improved and the structure of informal control exercised from the coast would once again become viable. Had such agreements gone through, the result would almost certainly have been to forestall the scramble for southern Africa that was to take place in the 1880s. However, the agreements ran into domestic difficulties before they were eventually wrecked on the reefs of international diplomacy.

Perversely, the principal objections came from the very interest groups for whose benefit the treaties had been devised. Manchester traders clamoured that Portugal would reintroduce her prohibitive tariffs once the treaties were signed, while opposition forces in Portugal claimed that the treaties would merely extend British financial and commercial control of the Portuguese colonies and would thwart the plans for a more independent national economy. It was characteristic of the period of the economic recession that set in around 1879 that different interests reacted to economic and political proposals in wholly different ways. Interest group was set against interest group in a way that made economic and political planning impossible.

The progress of the treaties was not helped by the continuing series of military and political disasters that overtook British policy in South Africa. After the Zulu War Britain tried to impose a limited form of indirect rule in Zululand but this soon broke down in civil war. In 1880 the Gun War broke out in Basutoland and in 1881 the Boers of the

Transvaal rebelled.   Rather than face prolonged strife in southern Africa, the new prime minister, Gladstone, decided once and for all to wind up the confederation policy and revert to a position where southern Africa remained politically divided but indirectly controlled by British commercial dominance – in other words to revert as far as possible to the policy of the 1860s.   The Transvaal was granted limited independence in 1882 and Basutoland was duly taken from the Cape and made an imperial protectorate in 1884.

## 12. The Scramble of the 1880s

It is conventional wisdom that what destroyed this fresh attempt at informal empire almost before it began, and what finally buried the Anglo-Portuguese treaties, was the wholly unexpected entry of Germany into the colonial field.   In 1882 no one had heard of Germany as a colonial power.   In late 1883, with certain trading and propaganda circles in Germany beginning to talk about empire, and with Reichstag elections in the offing, Bismarck decided to grant German protection to traders in south west Africa.   In a rapid series of moves early in 1884 Germany set up a protectorate over the whole south west African coast and moved into Tanganyika and the Cameroons.   Initially stunned by the pace of events, Britain hastily moved to secure her position in Bechuanaland and the critical areas of the east coast, while in February 1885 the Berlin congress finally tore up the Anglo-Portuguese Congo treaty and redrew the map of central Africa.   This scenario, in which all the initiatives appear to have come from Europe, ignores the local economic changes that were precipitating events – Bismarck or no Bismarck.(16)

Late in the 1870s movement had again begun among the pastoral societies of southern Africa.   Bands of armed Boers took their herds across the Kalahari into South West Africa and on into Angola, establishing themselves around Humpata in 1882.   Here their arrival set in motion a revolution in transport with Boer wagons opening up the trade of the interior in an unprecedented manner.   Cattle also began to be exported from southern Angola in large quantities in the 1880s.   At the same time Boers began to occupy grazing land on the eastern fringes of the Kalahari, setting up the republics of Stellaland and Goschen in 1883, and in 1884 founding the New Republic after a lucrative intervention in the Zulu civil wars.   The same period saw the massive alienation of Swazi pastureland to Boer immigrants.   By 1886 Boer pioneers were known to be examining the possibility of a major trek across the Limpopo into Mashonaland.

The economic causes of this expansion are not entirely clear. It may have been the result of the terrible droughts of the 1870s coming after a period when the hunting economy had been declining and game had been scarce, or it may have been linked to the growth of the poor white class.   By the 1870s most land within the Republics was owned by the heads of the powerful Boer clans who allowed their relatives and clients to squat as bywonners. The latter supplemented their living through marginal activities like transport, riding and hunting.   Much of the land in the Republics had also been bought up by land companies who found it more profitable to rent plots to African cultivators than to poor whites.   The rising market prices for food in the mining areas did not help the poor whites either, for they responded less flexibly to the

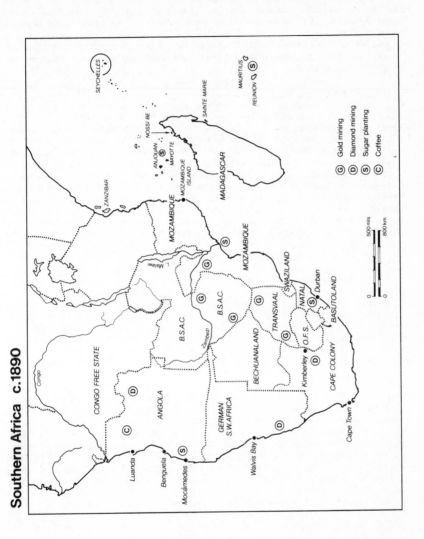

Southern Africa c.1890

market forces than their African counterparts. As in the 1820s and 1830s, the Boer frontiersman retained one asset - his skill with horse and gun - and rather than be driven further to the margins of poverty, large numbers once again began to trek. The movement of armed bands of Boers soon caused turmoil within African society and could not be ignored since, after 1883, the Germans threatened to provide 'protection' to groups not so protected by Britain.

Powerful interest groups were, at the same time, about to initiate their own local scramble for power in central Africa. Since the military disasters of the 1860s, the Portuguese had not tried to assert their authority on the Zambesi but had reverted to the traditional rule through capitaes-mores. These continued their slaving and ivory hunting, selling ivory to the Portuguese and slaves to the Arabs, or to Ndebele and Barotse chiefs. However, the Portuguese did manage to consolidate their control in the delta and encouraged a few plantation companies to start business. The Afro-Portuguese slavers did not possess the capital, the technology or the business contacts to develop the regions they dominated, while the Portuguese concessionaries on the coast could not expand their activities inland because of the lack of security. However, if the two interests could somehow come together an explosive mixture might result.

The late 1870s saw the rise in Zambesia of an Indian slaver and ivory trader called Manuel Antonio de Sousa. At first no different from the other Zambesi warlords, Sousa early realised the significance of the decline of Gaza power and appreciated the advantages to be gained by collaborating with the Portuguese government. By 1875 he was the trusted agent of Portuguese informal empire, receiving handouts of firearms and government backing for his own empire-building projects. In 1880 his private army seized the African chieftaincy of Barue and twice, in 1884 and 1887-8, Sousa lent his forces to aid the Portuguese in suppressing risings against their rule. In 1882 Sousa formed a pact with a Portuguese entrepreneur, Paiva de Andrada, who had obtained a large land concession from the Portuguese government. Unable to develop his concession, which lay largely outside Portuguese control, Andrada sought capital in vain. An alliance with Sousa would enable him to develop his concession, while Sousa saw in links with a bona fide European company the possibility of 'laundering' his ill-gotten gains and turning his conquests to account. Sousa's ambitions lay on the high veldt of Mashonaland and in 1886 he and Andrada launched the first of their attacks on the Shona chieftaincy of Mtoko. This was a military failure and in the subsequent two years Sousa concentrated his military activities on aiding the Portuguese governor to crush the most notorious of the slave trading dynasties, the da Cruz of Massangano.

In the wake of these purely local initiatives, the governments of Britain and Portugal followed with their diplomatic fire extinguishers, trying to dampen down the local bush fires and ultimately to achieve a new stability which would limit the commitment of the metropolitan tax payer and which would reestablish where possible an informal empire. So, in 1885-6, Britain was forced into intervention in Tswana territory in Zululand and Swaziland, while the Portuguese were forced to reach a settlement with the Boers who had trekked into southern Angola. These settlements largely accommodated the economic interests of the Boers who had precipitated the crisis. The land in the

New Republic, most of the land in Stellaland, Swaziland and the Humpata highlands was guaranteed in Boer possession, and by making these concessions Britain and Portugal bought a short span of peace and order. Between 1886 and 1888 Portugal also tried to establish her claims to the areas south of the Congo Free State, which had been created at Berlin, and north of the British sphere of influence – substantially the area that Portugal would have obtained under the defunct bilateral treaties. Official Portuguese expeditions were organised to all the principal areas where informal control through capitaes-mores had been the rule. These expeditions were equipped with draft treaties and flags and were to establish a Portuguese presence which would accord with the internationally accepted principles of 'effective occupation'. It was one of these expeditions, commanded by Serpa Pinto, to the Shire that triggered off Britain's ultimatum to Portugal in January 1890. However, this small incident assumed great significance only because economic changes had once again produced the fissile material for yet another local crisis.

13. Cecil Rhodes and the Capitalist Revolution

The discovery of the Witwatersrand goldfields in 1886 was in some ways merely an extension of the mining revolution which had begun at Lydenburg, Tati and Kimberley. Capital and immigrants flowed in from abroad, railway building increased, new ancillary industries were founded and massive amounts of labour had to be organised. Because these developments were really only an intensification of trends which began in the 1870s, their immediate impact was not so revolutionary. However, Rand capitalism soon developed its own peculiar dynamic which has only recently been fully investigated by historians. The early days of the Rand discoveries created a highly volatile market in gold shares where large fortunes could be made by insider trading. At the same time it became known that the gold bearing reef tilted at an angle and that many of the gold claims could only be exploited at deep levels which were highly expensive to work. Among those who held predominantly deep level claims were Cecil Rhodes and his associates. As Rhodes' gold investments held out no promise of immediate profit, his company was placed under great pressure to diversify or to speculate in order to bring short term dividends or speculative gains. Ever since the 1860s it had been known that there was workable gold north of the Limpopo and the fevered atmosphere of the Rand boom turned these rumours into an ill-founded assumption that there existed a new Rand to the north. It was Rhodes who had the resources, the entrepreneurship and the local political muscle which enabled him to lead all his rivals in exploiting this new region. In 1889 he obtained a charter for his new British South Africa Company (Chartered Company) and at once sent sent expeditions out to extend the sphere of its operations north of the Zambesi towards the copper bearing country of the upper Congo. Little was known at the time about the real resources of central Africa but Rhodes was concerned to gain a monopoly of mineral exploitation in the vast region between the Limpopo and the Congo and so pre-empt the rival mining syndicates which had successfully excluded him, so it seemed at the time, from enjoying the profits of the Rand.

Rhodesia turned out to be an investment even more speculative than the deep level mines on the Rand, and the pressures on Rhodes to provide finance for his new colonial territories and to safeguard his massive speculation were to lead him into a series of political actions dictated, if not by cold economic logic, at least by a gambler's determination to make good earlier losses. Each of these moves created, or threatened to create, a political crisis to which the government in Britain, ever anxious to restore stability in international relations, was forced to react. The founding of the Chartered Company on the flimsy prospectus of Rudd's dubious mining concession from king Lobengula of the Ndebele, was a brilliant political coup in which Lord Salisbury acquiesced because it appeared to resurrect the old policy of indirect rule – this time through a chartered mining company. Rhodes then, unilaterally, vastly extended the Company's sphere of activity by treaty-signing north of the Zambesi and by buying out the African Lakes Company. Again Whitehall acquiesced because Rhodes offered to pay the expenses of a protectorate at a time when the concept of a protectorate still seemed to mean little more than the traditional type of indirect rule smartened up for the sake of the susceptibilities of the Berlin Congress powers. However no sooner did Rhodes have his charter than he proceeded, in Southern Rhodesia at least, to turn his mining concession into a settler colony. The reason for this was his desperate need to realise assets other than the increasingly speculative gold mines. Land and labour were the obvious assets to exploit. To give the land at his disposal the added value necessary, Rhodes had to gain access to the sea and it was this consideration that lay behind his repeated attempts to carry out further coups at the expense of the Portuguese. In 1890, and again in 1891, the Foreign Office had to intervene to stop Rhodes filibustering into the area of Portuguese influence and upsetting the new Anglo-Portuguese treaty that Salisbury was trying to negotiate. Then in 1892 came the unfavourable reports on the gold reefs of Rhodesia and in an attempt to save the value of his investment Rhodes and Jameson led their brilliantly successful attack on the Ndebele in 1893 and seized control of Matabeleland – a coup which gave them vast new land resources to exploit and which boosted the sagging Chartered Company shares.

The twin problems of Rhodes' deep level investments on the Rand and his expensive, and so far profitless, investment in the Rhodesias was to lead him to precipitate yet another crisis at the end of the 1895 – a crisis which opened with the attempted coup in the Transvaal and Jameson's famous Raid, and which ended with the widespread African rebellion in Southern Rhodesia which was the result of the crudeness of Rhodes' administrative methods and the way in which he attempted to extract profit from the cattle, land and labour of the African inhabitants.(17)

14. Conclusion

At each stage it had been the intention of Whitehall to safeguard British interests in southern Africa in the cheapest and most informal way possible. Possession of the ports and coastline had been the traditional technique. To this was added after 1884 the loose protectorate agreements which covered, or barely covered, Swaziland, Basutoland and Bechuanaland and the protectorate that the government thought it had created to run the Rhodesias and Nyasaland through the agency of the Chartered Company. The Germans for their part had tried to turn their grandiose schutzgebiet, created by Bismarck in 1883-4, into a loose protectorate under a trading company, while the Portuguese had done the same, setting up the Mozambique Company in 1888 and the Niassa Company in 1893, trying at the same time to find commercial companies to administer Zambesia as well.

The 1890s saw the collapse of this attempt at holding the ratchet at a stage of inexpensive and informal empire. The Germans and Portuguese were overwhelmed by the local warfare and anarchy arising from attempts to impose an unworkable framework of protection on irreconcileable economic interests, while in the British sphere the arrangement was wrecked by the investment problems of Rhodes and his company's need to strengthen its finances.

# Notes

1. Figures in E.A. Alpers, 'The French Slave Trade in East Africa (1721-1810)', Cahiers d'Etudes Africaines, 37, 1970, pp.80-124; L. Vail and L. White, Capitalism and Colonialism in Mozambique (London, 1980) esp. chapter 1.

2. P. Harries, 'Slavery, Social Incorporation and Surplus Extraction; the Nature of Free and Unfree Labour in South-East Africa', Journal of African History, 22, 1981, pp.309-330.

3. G. Campbell, 'Labour and the Transport Problem in Imperial Madagascar, 1810-1895', Journal of African History, 21, 1980, pp.341-356.

4. For this explanation of Zulu raiding, see D. Hedges, 'Trade and Politics in Southern Mozambique', unpublished Ph.D. thesis, University of London, 1977.

5. W.G. Clarence-Smith, Slaves, Peasants and Capitalists in Southern Angola 1840-1926 (Cambridge, 1979) esp. chapters 5 and 6.

6. C. Bundy, The Rise and Fall of the South African Peasantry (London, 1979) chapters 2 and 3.

7. For the rubber boom and its impact, see Clarence-Smith, op.cit.; R. Austin and R. Headrick, 'Equatorial Africa under Colonial Rule' in D. Birmingham and P. Martin, History of Central Africa (2 vols., Harlow, 1983); H. Possinger, 'Interrelations between Economic and Social Change in Rural Africa: the case of the Ovimbundu of Angola' in edit. F. Heimer, Social Change in Angola (Munich, 1973).

AACA-E

8.  For the development of plantations in Angola, see Clarence-Smith, op.cit.; D. Birmingham, 'The Coffee Barons of Cazengo', Journal of African History, 24, 1978, pp.523-538; Jill Dias, 'Black Chiefs, White Traders and Colonial Policy near the Kwanza: Kabuku Ambilo and the Portuguese, 1873-1896', Journal of African History, 17, 1976, pp.245-265.

9.  M. Newitt, The Comoro Islands (Boulder, 1984) esp. chapter 2; P.M. Mutibwa, The Malagasy and the Europeans (Harlow, 1974) esp. chapter 2.

10. Jill Dias, 'Famine and Disease in the History of Africa c.1830-1930', Journal of African History, 22, 1981, pp.349-378; J.C. Miller, 'The Significance of Drought, Disease and Famine in the agriculturally marginal zones of West-Central Africa', Journal of African History, 23, 1982, pp.17-31.

11. N. Parsons, 'The Economic History of Khama's Country in Botsawana, 1844-1930', in R. Palmer and N. Parsons, The Roots of Rural Poverty (London, 1977) pp.113-143.

12. S. Marks and A. Atmore, 'The Imperial Factor in South Africa in the Nineteenth Century: towards a Reassessment', Journal of Imperial and Commonwealth History, 3, 1974, pp.105-139.

13. M. Newitt, Portuguese Settlement on the Zambesi (Harlow, 1973).

14. R. Wagner, 'Zoutpansberg: the Dynamics of a Hunting Frontier' in edit. S. Marks and A. Atmore, Economy and Society in Pre-industrial South Africa (Harlow, 1980) pp. 313-349; P. Delius, 'Migrant Labour and the Pedi, 1840-1880', in ibid., pp.293-312.

15. J. Guy, The Destruction of the Zulu Kingdom (Harlow, 1979).

16. For a recent restatement of the traditional view, see D.M. Schreuder, The Scramble for Southern Africa (Cambridge, 1980).

17. R. Mendelsohn, 'Blainey and the Jameson Raid: the Debate Renewed', Journal of South African Studies, 7, 1980, pp.157-270; I.R. Phimister, 'Rhodes, Rhodesia and the Rand', ibid., 1, 1974, pp.74-90.

# Russian Expansion into Central Asia

## PETER MORRIS

The modern history of Russian expansion into central Asia began during the 1840s when military detachments penetrated the hitherto autonomous kirgiz steppelands south of the customs and defence lines established in 1730, which ran along the Ural river from its efflux into the Caspian Sea to Orenburg, Orsk, Petro-Pavlovsk, Semipalatinsk and on to the Chinese frontier (see map 1). By 1887 the entire area between that line and the present-day north eastern frontier of Iran and northern frontier of Afghanistan had been occupied (see map 2). It comprised the present Kazakh, Kirgiz, Uzbek, Turkmen and Tadzhik Soviet Socialist Republics and embraced over 1,500,000 square miles, or more than seven times the area of France. The process involved wars with the independent khanates of Kokand, Khiva and Bokhara, all predominantly settled and relatively densely populated. They were states whose shadowy frontiers and precarious stability belied their glittering reputations as great centres of islamic civilisation. The first was entirely liquidated and its territories absorbed into the Empire in 1876. The second and third retained their formal independence until 1920, though in 1873 Bokhara lost its wealthy northern fringes, including the important cities of Tashkent and Samarcand, the former becoming the capital of the governor-generalship of Turkestan, established in 1867. The desert lands east of the Caspian Sea were absorbed during the 1870s and 1880s when their independent nomadic and anarchic turcoman inhabitants were defeated by military expeditions and their elders persuaded to accept Russian suzerainty. Merv, now known as Mary, was absorbed in 1884 and Russian troops entered territories claimed by the amir of Afghanistan. The clash between Russian and Afghan troops at Panjdeh in March 1885 led to a diplomatic crisis between Russia and Britain, since 1879 in control of Afghan foreign relations. In 1887 the present-day Russo-Afghan frontier was finally delimited, that with Iran having been largely negotiated in 1881. Apart from the later frontier delimitation in the Pamir Mountains in 1894 Russia had acquired her present-day central Asian territories.

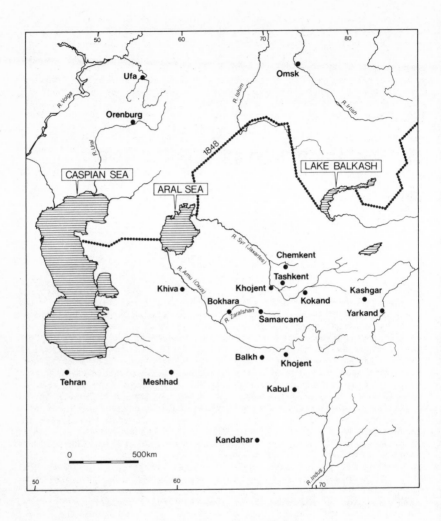

Russia in Central Asia, 1840

Soviet attitudes toward this annexation have varied greatly. For an earlier generation of historians, the most eminent of whom was M.N. Pokrovsky, it was a clear example of classic nineteenth century imperialism. During the past twenty-five years however a consensus has formed that it was the desirable and progressive consequence of the emergence of capitalistic economic forces within the Imperial Russian economy. This view has been elaborated in particular by the school of historians led by N.A. Khalfin, whose major work Politika Rossii v Sredney Azii published in 1960 is available in an abridged English translation.(1) Attempts at reinterpretation by, most notably, M.K. Rozhkova who has argued against too great a reliance on purely economic causation, have largely been ignored. Along with the emancipation of the serfs after 1861 it is argued expansion in central Asia reflected the presence within the Empire of a strong upward thrust of capitalist development. It is further evidence that the 'bourgeois' phase of economic development had progressed sufficiently far for its evolution into the dictatorship of the proletariat and is thus further evidence for the legitimacy in marxist terms of the 1917 Revolution. By removing capitalism, the latter removed all taint of imperialist exploitation from Russia's relationship with her central Asian territories.(2) Whatever the short-term disadvantages, central Asia had been brought by tsarist armies into the mainstream of the modern economic world and its inhabitants exposed to the beneficial effects of progress, whilst in the longer-term the peoples of the region were associated with the benefits of the socialist revolution, otherwise unobtainable. By definition, therefore, the concept of imperialism is deemed inappropriate.

Determined though intermittent efforts had been made by successive Imperial Russian governments since the time of Peter the Great to bring central Asia under the aegis of Russia. Attracted by the possibilities of resuscitating and developing the traditional overland trade routes linking Europe with the East, and especially with China and India, Peter had sought to develop and strengthen such connections by treaty arrangements with the khan of Khiva who, seeking to bolster his position against revolted subjects, offered his submission to the tsar. It was not until 1717 that the first governmental expedition was sent from St Petersburg, under Prince A. Bekovich-Cherkassky. It was wiped out by a Khivan khan who had repented of his original bargain. Thereafter official links with the region effectively lapsed as the Imperial government adopted a defensive posture, symbolised in the construction of the customs and defence lines by which it strove to control contacts with central Asia.

In the early years of the nineteenth century the position began to change. Russia's economic position deteriorated as after 1815 an increasing torrent of cheaply produced British manufactured goods steadily encroached upon markets traditionally dominated by Russia. By the 1830s it was ousting Russian goods from the Ottomann Empire and, despite all the advantages of territorial propinquity, threatened Russian textile and metal goods exports to northern Iran. The trend had become apparent in the early years of the reign of Alexander I and from 1802 special committees in St Petersburg had intermittently wrestled with the problems of sustaining Russian trade with central Asia. That it was necessary to look to this region at all was an admission of economic weakness. As the ministry of finance stated in its annual report for 1817

> In the West Russia borders on states more
> developed than we in industrial relationships,
> and therefore only in the East can our factories
> and workshops find a guaranteed sale for their
> products. On the other hand, the development of
> trade with Asia is important in political terms
> as one way of bringing close to us and of
> pacifying savage Asiatic tribes (3)

emphasising the point very neatly. The objectives of enhancing exporting possibilities and of advancing political objectives were linked. In the Petrine tradition the Imperial government did not hold laissez-faire economic principles and saw little difference between economic and political desiderata. Its interest was part of the wider objective of securing outlets for Russian manufactured products and strengthening Russia's part in the international transit trade. Both were to come under increasingly heavy pressure as competition from British manufactured goods, carried by seaborne trade, steadily undermined Russia's position. In response, the Imperial government sought to strengthen the traditional land trade-routes which had made Astrakhan and Nizhni-Novgorod into major international trading centres through their links with Bokhara, described by a contemporary British Indian official as

> centrically placed for the trade between Eastern
> and Western Asia. Situated almost on the edge of
> the Russian steppes, it is a convenient entrepôt
> for merchandise brought from the south (4)

and to secure guaranteed markets for the products of increasingly obsolescent Russian manufacturing processes. However as the nineteenth century progressed, Russia's international trading position continued to decline. From being the world's major exporter of pig-iron in the final quarter of the eighteenth century she had become a net importer by the 1830s. The concern of the Imperial government accordingly grew. As the pendulum swung against Russian exports in traditional Asiatic markets the Chinese Empire became the major market for Russian manufactured goods, accounting for well over 60% of all Russian exports to Asia during the 1840s. Yet by the end of the decade increasing pressures from seaborne trade were threatening Russian goods there, too. The overland route was slow and expensive. Transport costs from Nizhni Novgorod to Bokhara, for example, averaged 1 rubl per pud (36 lbs) weight whilst local currencies lacked a fixed standard or established weight. The difficulties of transit trade through none too stable muslim khanates, where anti-christian fanaticism was always liable to break out, were added complications. Finally the outbreak of muslim anti-Chinese rebellion in Sinkiang in 1862 cut trade routes with the heartlands of the Chinese Empire. It was particularily disconcerting to find that the eventual leader of that uprising, Yakub Beg, had in 1853 led the troops of the amir of Kokand in their defence of the fortress of Ak Mechet on the river Syr against Russian forces. The continuing decline in exports aroused the attention not only of the Government but also of such public opinion as existed within the Empire. It led A.A. Semenov to chart it in his Studies in the Historical Information on Russian Foreign Trade from the mid seventeenth century until 1858, published in 1859. It also encouraged British officials. As J.S. Lumley, secretary at the British embassy at St Petersburg reported in January 1861

> Russian woollens, cottons and hardware, hitherto
> supplied to Central Asia, are declining in favour
> under the development of trade, civilisation and
> riches, and...in time they will probably succumb
> under increased competition with British
> manufactures. (5)

As in so many other aspects of Russian life, the Crimean War was a catalyst. The sharp pangs of defeat required the re-assertion of Russian self-esteem. Military and economic weakness were closely intertwined and galvanised the government into a wide-ranging internal reorganisation and aggressive fostering of its economic potential. Despite Soviet claims to the contrary, it is striking how small a part was played by private capitalists. Far from reflecting the burgeoning growth of Russia's economy, official anxieties testified to the reverse. Calls for action to encourage trade with central Asia came from orientalists such as Berezin, representatives of the ministry of marine, such as Butyrkin or academics, such as Grigor'ev, not from capitalists.

To these enthusiastic exponents of a drive to control central Asian trade the realities must have been discouraging. During the 1840s and 1850s trade with the region was either in the hands of central Asiatic muslim merchants, subjects of the khanates, who travelled to fairs within the empire and traded there with their Russian counterparts, or of Russian subjects who belonged not to the ranks of the merchants but to the peasantry or the meshchanstvo, the lowest officially designated urban estate, comprising pedlars or petty merchants liable to poll-tax and to conscription. Most of the latter were muslim tatars, for whom it was easier to live amongst and trade with their co-religionists. If anything the record before the Crimean War suggested that such Russian merchants as had been trading with the central Asian khanates were pulling out and leaving the field to their native rivals. This was despite the desire of Imperial officials to encourage their fellow countrymen. The total volume of Russian exports was small. In the eighteen years between 1840 and 1857 they averaged less than 15% of those to China and ran at slightly more than 900,000 rubls annually. Less than half consisted of the cotton goods so often claimed to be the single most important Russian export to the region, and their value was exceeded by that of imported cheap native cotton goods of durable quality, especially from Bokhara. The market for metallic household articles was probably more important and Russian knives, nails, samovars, pitchers and needles found a ready welcome. Certainly the total proportion of all Russian exports which found its way to the khanates was small, less than 1% in 1857, even if for certain products it had a disproportionate importance.

Whilst there was little or no impetus to territorial expansion in the region from the commercial and industrial community, once the area had been annexed or reduced to clientage there was an immediate, substantial development of Russian trade. The regularisation of relations centred about the conclusion of commercial conventions: with Kokand in December 1868, and as part of the peace treaties with Khiva in August and with Bokhara in September 1873. In each case discriminatory taxes and tariffs levied on Russian subjects were to be abolished and they were to be assured free and safe passage. Trade increased considerably. Between 1857 and 1867 trade over the Asiatic frontier of the Empire grew from 7.2% of total exports to 10.6% and more than doubled in value. Truly spectacular was the increase in exports to the khanates. In 1857 they amounted to 1,164,000 <u>rubls</u>. Ten years later they stood at 10,275,000 or more than 40% of Asiatic trade, compared with less than 10% in 1857. Exports to China meanwhile had declined from over half to less than 20% of the Empire's Asiatic trade, and by one third in total value. Particularily striking was the rapid surge in trade through Tashkent. Exports of cotton goods grew quickly and by 1867 accounted for 70% of the total. Whilst the discontinuation of the collection of trade statistics on the erstwhile Asiatic frontier of Russia after 1867 made later comparisons and the calculation of subsequent trends almost impossible, occasional evidence suggests that the strong upward trend may well have levelled off at the 1867 figure. Thus evidence from Tashkent suggests that the level of exports from Russia in 1874 was if anything below that of 1867, suggesting there may have been a pent-up demand for Russian goods which the conquest released.(6)

Most striking of all was the increase in imports to Russia of raw cotton, long produced in the well watered oases of the khanates and imported thence to the mills of European Russia and of the kingdom of Poland. While the increase may have owed something to the success of Russian arms, it owed even more to the American Civil War which by disrupting the international cotton trade deprived the Russian industry of its raw materials. That an alternative source of supply was available to the Empire's cotton industry was the outcome of an unusually happy coincidence of military activity and commercial demand. Between 1840 and 1860 total requirements of Russian industry had risen from about 400,000 to nearly 2,840,000 <u>puds</u> annually, and well over 90% of this had come from the U.S.A. With the onset of civil war imports in 1862 fell to less than one quarter of the 1861 figure whilst those from central Asia grew from 151,756 to over 400,000 <u>puds</u>. From just over 5% of Russia's raw cotton needs, central Asia provided over half of the admittedly much smaller figure for 1863. Even after the end of the Civil War, when shipments resumed from the U.S.A., the total central Asian supply continued to increase, reaching over three quarters of a million <u>puds</u> in 1867, when it represented over 22% of total Russian requirements. The increase in six years had been fourfold.

Whilst this surge in trade may have been welcomed, it was by no means independently generated. The Imperial government went to considerable lengths to foster interest in the new opportunities. In particular, the creation of new organisations to trade with central Asia owed much to governmental initiative. The Moscow-Tashkent Trading Company, established in December 1865 and headed by the leading Moscow merchant A.I. Khludov, had a considerable governmental input, represented on its Board by councillor of state V.I. Butovsky. It had been created as a consequence of the initiative of local military commanders in Tashkent, one of whom, general Romanovsky, visited Moscow and convened meetings there with leading merchants. The statutes of the company were based on those brought by Romanovsky. A similar military initiative brought major-general A.I. Gomzin to Moscow in January 1871 to meet leading silk manufacturers. He persuaded them to set up another Moscow-Tashkent Company, this time devoted to fostering cooperation amongst silk manufacturers. The tsar approved it in May 1871. Once more Butovsky was instrumental in securing the cooperation of leading

Moscow merchants, one of whom, Timofei Morozov, became chairman of the new body. In fact neither company prospered. Undercapitalised and not particularily active, they testified to the government's capacity to twist arms but not to initiate successful trading ventures. The horses, driven to water, did not seem thirsty. The real hopes for trade with central Asia and for boosting Russian exports lay with those who had dominated the trade previously, peasants and meshchaniye from the Volga provinces and from the guberniyas of Ufa and Orenburg. As Pokrovsky wrote in 1933

> In the long run the conquest of Central Asia proved of tremendous importance for the development of Russian industry. The country became Russia's first colonial possession.... But the importance of Central Asia was not at first realized. The catch seemed poor.(7)

The relative lack of success of official initiatives did not dampen the enthusiasm of military and civil officials for the commercial and trading prospects offered by central Asia. They continually reported on the great opportunities which they saw opening up. Successive military measures on the eastern shore of the Caspian Sea, beginning with the establishment of a base at Krasnovodsk in 1869, were justified in part by commercial arguments, as were those against the turcomans, culminating in the annexation of Merv in 1884 and the crisis over the delimitation of the northern frontier of Afghanistan. A special conference in 1865 decided military measures were needed to spread Russia's 'moral influence' over the tribesmen and to develop trade through Krasnovodsk. Two suitable merchants were identified: V.A. Kokorev, the prime mover in the Transcaspian Trading Company, officially approved in June 1857 after active lobbying by officials from the Caucasus, and a merchant from Astrakhan named Saval'ev. There was however little objective evidence to encourage hopes. Trading organisations operating through Astrabad had petered out in the mid-1840s and during the peak trading season at Krasnovodsk between October 1870 and March 1871 total transactions amounted to no more than 46,000 rubls. Even so, all subsequent military advances were justified in the name of trade. Grand duke Michael, viceroy in the Caucasus, emphasised in his reports that great commercial advantages were to be gained, whilst general Lomakin, whose two defeats at the hands of the turcomans in 1877 and 1879 won him the palm of least successful Russian general in central Asia, argued that trade with the transcaspian region was on the point of developing. A permanent fort located on the river Atrek would, he claimed, become a great trading centre.

Military men continued to proclaim hopes of economic advantage. General K.P. fon-Kaufman, first governor-general of Turkestan between 1867 and 1882 tried hard to foster the region's economic potential(8) whilst general Rosenbakh, the third governor-general confided to state secretary Polovtsov in November 1888

> Tashkent has a great economic future and he, Rosenbakh, is making every effort to develop peacefully the resources of this area, avoiding any military clashes or complications. Cotton, wine, fruit - these are the products which Tashkent will deliver to Russia in abundance.(9)

Similar enthusiasms were shared by non-Russians such as Sir H.C. Rawlinson, the leading British authority on the area, whose book England and Russia in the East appeared in 1875. At the same time the deserts of Transcaspia were proving less fruitful than earlier enthusiasts had claimed, and it was not suprising that general Komarov was thought to wish to take possession of the fertile areas of neighbouring Afghanistan and Iran. Once more soldiers proclaiming economic possibilities urged military action.

Such claims were of course greatly exaggerated. When military men spoke of economic opportunities and tried to promote action by reluctant investors and traders they had more in mind than profit. It may be true as the Iranian scholar Kazemzadeh has suggested that

> It had become the fashion in the nineteenth century to justify aggressive action, interference in the internal affairs of nations, and even war, by the supposed interests of commerce. Industry and trade had been raised to the status of gods in the new bourgeois mythology.(10)

but it was not only, or even mainly, the bourgeoisie which used such justifications. They were every bit as popular amongst soldiers. For them however trade was a form of cold war and the attempts made in 1841 and 1842 to drive Russian cotton goods from Bokhara by flooding the market with cheap British items must have confirmed their prejudices. The successful penetration of British products into central Asia and the osmosis which seemed to draw that market into the orbit of British India must have seemed an insidious danger. The battle between British and Russian goods for dominance attracted the attention of many civilians who also saw it as a political rather than a commercial battle. Sir Alexander Burnes's record of travels to Bokhara, the observations of the secretary to the American legation, Eugene Schuyler, or of his fellow-countryman, Macgahan, contained much material on the relative trading positions of the two powers. For Russians, the threat on the field of trade had to be met. The experiences of events in the Ottomann Empire, Iran and China suggested commerce could not be left to its own devices. Officials felt they must foster it and shoe-horn reluctant capitalists into it. Given the tradition of state intervention in economic affairs, the close control over trading enterprises and the pervasive oversight by officials, entrepreneurs would usually respond to official encouragement.

Such patriotic attitudes might merge with more personal considerations. Some commanders sought concessions, usually for communications works. General M.G. Cherniaev, involved in speculative promotions of railway lines in European Russia, linked up in 1870 with Severtsov and two other prominent Moscow merchants to promote river communications in central Asia. The 1873 slump ended these adventures and left him heavily in debt. Contemporaries often fiercely criticised fon-Kaufman's failure to stamp out financial irregularities amongst his subordinates. There seems to have been some truth in these claims, for army officers in central Asia were often closely involved in securing contracts for public works even if overall the allegations were exaggerated. As the protégé of the war minister, D.A. Milyutin, Kaufman often stood proxy for the latter in personal and political attacks. It was not suprising that passions ran high between Cherniaev and his supporters and Kaufman and those around him. Milyutin had secured the former's dismissal for exceeding his orders in 1865 and had then ensured Kaufman's appointment as compensation for his removal from the governorship of Vilna. Despite the vituperation there was little difference in their attitudes, as Cherniaev was to show whilst second governor-general of Turkestan between 1882 and 1884.

Campaigns in central Asia were extremely attractive for restless soldiers. They were a natural extension of the campaigns in the Caucasus, where the subduing of the muslim hillsmen under Shamyl rendered idle the large military forces there. Prince A.I. Bariatinsky, viceroy between 1857 and 1864, sought to add to his command the governorship of Astrakhan and the troops around the Aral Sea. Rebuffed, he and his successor the grand duke Michael successfully sought to ensure that military operations on the eastern shore of the Caspian Sea came under their aegis. Military success brought individuals medals, promotion, fame as for example the career of major-general Abramof showed. As the German ambassador von Schweinitz remarked of the rewards heaped on Skobelev after his victory at Geok-Teppeh in 1881

> The double reward - the Cross of St George and
> the rank of full general - stands in no
> relationship whatsoever to the tactically
> insignificant victory over people lacking
> firearms.(11)

The risks involved were small. Russian casualties were extremely light, native ones crushingly heavy and often vitiated by wholesale massacres after battles. Almost invariably figures for native casualties were unobtainable. The storming of Khojent in 1866 cost the Russians five dead and 122 wounded whilst the defenders were estimated to have lost 2,500 men. Victory over Khiva was followed by a bloody pursuit and massacre of fleeing turcoman tribesmen who had tried too hard to defend themselves and Skobelev's storming of Geok-Teppeh in 1881 was followed by prolonged pursuit of panic-striken tribesmen fleeing with their women and children into the desert. Thousands were slain on both occasions, and Skobelev subsequently admitted that on the second over 20,000 turcomans had been killed for the loss of 283 Russians killed and 689 wounded. Campaigns in central Asia were fashionable. The elaborately prepared one against Khiva attracted fashionable guards officers from St Petersburg, amongst them grand duke Nicholas Constantinovich, the tsar's nephew, and prince Eugene of Leuchtenberg. It was difficult for the Imperial government to disavow success, for the dramatic advances of the armies increased the Empire's prestige and did something to re-burnish its military reputation. Although it protested its innocence of annexationary intent there was not a single example of conquered territory being surrendered.

Such career ambitions and personal aspirations augmented political considerations as the clash between Russia and Britain in Asia, long foreshadowed, became a reality in the 1850s. During the Crimean War talk in Britain of extending the conflict to the Caucasus and of arousing muslim sentiment against Russia coupled with the activities of free-lance Russophobes such as David Urquhart suggested

British competition was strengthening. In the new competitive atmosphere Russian memories of earlier British emissaries' visits to central Asia were reawakened. Visits to Bokhara by Moorcroft in 1824, Burnes in 1832, Stoddart in 1838, Connolly in 1841 and Wolff in 1844 and of Abbott and Shakespear to Khiva in 1840 were testimony to British interest in the region. Yet at the same time the Indian mutiny in 1857 and the ensuing long and savage re-conquest of India suggested that the British position was insecure. Not only did this seriously shake British self-confidence: it encouraged Russian ambitions. For Bariatinsky, events in India justified his view of the fragile basis of the British position. For him and for those who thought as he did Russia's moment had come. By advancing the Empire's boundaries the British threat could be snuffed out and an advance post for menacing gestures against India established. The accuracy of this analysis was confirmed during the crisis of 1877-8 when a Russian force of 20,000 men was moved to Djam. Interestingly, Soviet authors still regard the thwarting of British ambitions in central Asia as one of the major achievements of their Imperial forefathers.

With the accession of Alexander II in 1855 control over the Empire passed into the hands of a new generation. Aggressive and nationalistic, the new men were closely connected. Around Bariatinsky there gathered many of the leading actors of the new decade. His chief-of-staff from 1857 until 1861 was D.A. Milyutin, minister of war between 1861 and 1881. Another close associate and protégé was the panslav, anti-German general R.A. Fadeev, and it was perhaps in the Caucasian military district under Bariatinsky that most of the attitudes and assumptions of later nineteenth century expansion were incubated. Milyutin was a strong nationalist and bitterly anti-British. His brother, N.A. Milyutin, was largely responsible for the details of the 1861 emancipation and as his conduct in Poland after the 1863 rising showed, he too had a strong streak of Russian chauvinism. Another Bariatinsky protégé was N.P. Ignat'ev who headed a diplomatic mission to Khiva and Bokhara in 1858 before becoming successively military attaché in London and head of the Asiatic department of the ministry of foreign affairs from 1861 until 1864. He then became ambassador at Constantinople during the troubled 1870s and finally minister of the interior under Alexander III between 1881 and 1882. He was a classmate and friend of M.G. Cherniaev who during the 1870s collaborated closely with Fadeev and supported Bariatinsky's opposition to aspects of the military reform. Kaufman as already noted was a protégé of Milyutin. Given the relatively small size of the governing groups of the Empire these connections were not surprising. What was noteworthy was their relative unanimity on Asiatic matters. Imperial expansion in central Asia was an integral part of the political attitudes of the Empire's ruling elite after 1856. There was no debate over ends or objectives, though there were divisions over the pace and intensity, and especially over personnel matters. Who was to pick the plums? This commitment formed one of the bedrocks of the attitudes of the Empire's policy-makers and at its most extreme merged into panslavism, joining the Asiatic and Balkan interests of Russia into a common foreign policy programme.

Increasing internal trouble made it even more important that the willpower, enthusiasm and morale of supporters of autocracy be maintained. The only truly reliable support was the army. It met the challenge of internal unrest during and after emancipation, put down armed uprising in Poland with the attendant guerrilla war in 1864 and 1865 and policed an increasingly turbulent internal situation as the wave of opposition associated with the 'going to the people' movement and 'black partition' terrorist group seemed to threaten the very basis of the autocratic system. Four attempts on the life of Alexander II, ending in his assassination in March, 1881 were the most dramatic illustrations of the seriousness of the crisis.

After 1861 it was no longer possible to rely unquestioningly upon the landed gentry, traditional upholders of the tsarist system. Emancipation had been enacted against their sullen hostility and seriously damaged their economic and social predominance. Thereafter the government of Alexander II was unwilling or unable to place total reliance on them. Instead the role of the civil bureaucracy was enhanced as its control over all aspects of national administrative and governmental life expanded, whilst that of the military was confirmed. It seems clear that the Imperial government perceived this to be inadequate and that a new consensus had to be moulded which would attract and ensure the future support of sections of the wider public, albeit drawn from the numerically tiny ranks of the educated and propertied. This need gave influence and significance to such new men as the publicist M.N. Katkov and the jurist and imperial tutor K.P. Pobedonostsev. They and others like them shared strongly anti-democratic and anti-modern attitudes, laid almost mystical stress on the inheritance of Russian national tradition and, in the case of the Pobedonostsev, on orthodoxy as the religion of state and nation.

The programme of Asiatic expansion fitted this newly emerging conservatism, and was warmly embraced in 1881 by the new tsar Alexander III who, whilst tsarevich, had personally been close to panslav organisations acting for example as patron of the Moscow Slavonic Benevolent Committee. Arguably it continued until the shattering events of 1904-5 revealed the relative lack of success of this effort to construct a conservative bloc in support of autocracy and ushered in a new attempt to underpin it by Stolypin's wager on the strong. There have been many studies of late nineteenth century Imperial conservatism, notably by Rogger and Thaden as well as by the Soviet historian Zaionchkovsky (12), and the importance of central Asian expansion in it has been noted by Walicki amongst others

> [along with other developments of the 1860s] the colonization of Central Asia paved the way for the transformation of the conservative-romantic nationalism of the Slavophiles into a chauvinist nationalism that welcomed industrialization and urbanization if only as forces that would consolidate the political prestige of the empire and facilitate its expansion.(13)

During the late nineteenth century officials emerged in important positions within the Empire who had made their careers in central Asia. One such was I.A. Zinov'ev who after studying oriental languages had served in Iran between 1876 and 1883 where he had worked closely with Skobelev. He then moved to the ministry of foreign affairs, where from 1883 to 1891 he was director of the Asiatic department. Many Imperial

generals cut their professional teeth in central Asia. The best example
was general A.N. Kuropatkin, whose career began with service in the 1868
campaign against Samarcand. After serving briefly in Algeria he was back
in Kashgar in 1876 and 1877 before joining Skobelev in the Balkans. He
returned thence to serve in Turkestan and Transcaspia between 1879 and
1882. After eight years away from the region he was from 1890 until
1898 commander of Transcaspia before becoming minister of war in 1898.
As important as this cadre of officials was the creation of new heroes,
the darlings of public opinion, whose exploits indirectly contributed to
the security of the regime. Probably the best example was M.D.
Skobelev, whose brief career encompassed both central Asia and the
Balkans, where he served with distinction in the 1877 war. He became a
folk hero.(14) Something similar was true of Cherniaev, whose central
Asian exploits brought his name before the public eye. His subsequent
acquisition and editorship of the newspaper Russkii Mir helped keep him
prominent. Both prepared the ground for his much publicised command of
the eastern Serbian armies in the war with the Ottomann Empire in
1876.(15) The relationship between generals and their government was
often uneasy: the hero might become a political menace, as did both
Cherniaev and Skobelev. Yet it was impossible to disavow him. After
the 1885 Panjdeh clash a major stumbling block for the peaceful
resolution of the crisis was the British demand for an enquiry to
determine whether local commanders had acted in accordance with their
instructions. The Imperial government found it quite impossible to
accede. As Polovtsov noted in his diary, it was this demand for an
enquiry into Komarov's conduct which provoked the greatest indignation
at St Petersburg. Before becoming commander of Russian troops in the
transcaspian district, A.V. Komarov had made his career in the Caucasus.
His brother V.V. Komarov, editor and owner of the ultra-nationalist
newspaper Svet, had been associated with Cherniaev's Russkii Mir of
which he had been founder in 1871 and had served with that general in
the Balkans.

Whereas during the 1820s and 1830s the Caucasus had fired the
imagination of the artistic world and inspired for example Pushkin and
Lermontov, in the 1860s and 1870s central Asia did. Amongst others the
painter and writer V.V. Vereshchagin travelled in central Asia for
subject matter and local colour, his Autobiographical Sketches being
subsequently translated into English.(16) Asia provided material for
the composer Borodin. The news of the storming of the turcoman
stronghold of Geok-Teppeh led Dostoevsky to lyricise in his Diary for
1881 on the significance of Asia for Russia. In this unique, one-man
monthly magazine he joyously commented

> Asia, our Asiatic Russia, – why this is also our
> sick root, which has to be not only refreshed but
> resurrected and transformed. A principle, a new
> principle, a new vision of the matter – that is
> what we need.(17)

Nationalist sentiment, humiliated by the Crimean War and affronted by
the experiences of the Russo-Turkish war and the congress of Berlin saw
successes in central Asia as indicating a new departure in Russian
self-assertion and for her civilising mission. Like other imperialist
powers, Russia claimed to be an agent of civilisation. The official
attitude already framed earlier in the nineteenth century was given its

Russia in Central Asia, 1890

classical expression by M.D. Gorchakov in his circular dispatch of 1864to Russia's representatives abroad

> It always happens...that the interests of frontier security and of commercial relations demand the more civilised state exert a certain ascendancy over neighbours whose nomadic, turbulent habits make them very disagreeable... all [European states with imperial possessions] have inevitably been constrained to follow this progressive path. Ambition plays a lesser role than imperious necessity and the greatest difficulty lies in knowing how to stop.

This argument was given added weight by the slaving of the turcomans whose raids took them deep into Iran and Afghanistan but on occasion also into Russia.(18) It was perhaps symptomatic of the camaraderie of international imperialism that such claims were accepted even by anti-Russian Englishmen.

Travellers and explorers complemented soldiers and the artistic world. The urge to map and describe new regions hitherto un-visited was as apparent in Imperial Russia as it was in any other European state. Founded in 1845, the Imperial Russian Geographical Society set itself the objective of identifying such regions and sponsoring expeditions to them. Its long-time president and driving force, P.P. Semenov, made his reputation by explorations in the Tian-Shan range in Russian and Chinese Turkestan and throughout a long life continued to be particularily interested in central Asia.(19) The society often worked closely with the war ministry, especially under Milyutin whose scholarly interests happily combined with his political objectives. For example, the most famous Russian explorer, N.P. Prezhevalsky, made his first important journey between 1870 and 1873 under the auspices of the society and with the financial assistance of the war ministry.(20) Such explorations were worth governmental sponsorship, for in addition to contributing to scientific knowledge they made available topographical and other information of military use and performed a useful political function in showing the flag and familiarising native peoples with the presence and potential of Russia. Interestingly enough, in this as in other aspects of central Asian penetration it was the foreign ministry which was most reluctant to underwrite new activities, anxious as it was to maintain good relations with foreign powers and avoid diplomatic crises and complications.

With central Asia absorbed and British influence in Afghanistan acknowledged, territorial acquisitions ended, though Russian officials on the frontier did not hesitate to press the case for boundary revision, alleging the superiority of direct Russian rule over that of native khans and the need to maintain Russian prestige. Such suggestions were resisted in the interests of native rulers, whose prestige would, it was feared, suffer should they be implemented.(21) There seem to have been few immediate changes in the economy, society or organisational structure of the region certainly in the two decades after Russian absorption. Indeed Cherniaev whilst second governor-general made determined efforts to eradicate such innovations as had been made by his predecessor. He closed Kaufman's silk-worm breeding school and model cotton farm, and his chemical laboratory and libraries, dispersing their contents. Tentative steps to introduce Russian-style laws and regulations were abruptly ended. Tashkent itself remained a traditional central Asian city. Another, Russian city was developed alongside it, the population of which had reached 3000 by 1873. In the early 1880s this had grown to about 6,000. It was however a purely administrative and military city, not a commercial one. It continued steadily to increase, reaching 20,000 in 1889 and by 1910 it had over 47,000 inhabitants. However a commercial community only appeared during the 1890s.

This dual pattern of settlement, paralleled in other urban centres in the region, was characteristic of Russian central Asia until 1914. The region was treated much as the British treated India. Basic social and economic structures were left intact, with for example the crucial system of water gathering and distribution, upon which the prosperity of the area depended, being in the hands of the traditional controllers, using traditional methods. Only on the eve of the First World War was a comprehensive change in the laws governing irrigation in Russian Turkestan elaborated, and it was shelved on the outbreak of hostilities. Ownership of land had meanwhile been vested in the community of those who worked it, thus establishing something of the same sort of communal ownership as existed in European Russia after 1861. This confirmed the position of the native populations as owners of the land, rendering the influx of Russian settlers even less likely. The life-style of the nomadic populations of Transcaspia remained largely unaffected before 1914. So far as Bokhara and Khiva were concerned the impact of Russia was minimal. The native ruling families were left in place, paradoxically enjoying greater security of tenure as a result of military defeat than they had before. Thus on the death of Muzaffar ed-Din in 1885 the customary unrest and instability normal in Asiatic systems of government on the death of the ruler was avoided and Abd al-Ahad moved easily into his father's place, aided in no small part by the prompt recognition of the Russian governor-general of Turkestan and by demonstrative military gestures of support. Until 1914 the repressive and extortionate demands of Bokharan rulers were a by-word amongst Russians, some of whom favoured direct annexation. Imperial policy however was to leave things as they were, interfering but little in the internal affairs of the khanate so long as Russia's requirements were promptly met. So long as the native, ruling elite kept order, avoided trouble and was obedient to Russian interests the Imperial government was content to leave it in control. European attitudes gradually percolated into the khanate through Russian officials and traders or through the personnel of the railway line which crossed Bokharan territory on its way from Merv to Samarcand, and by 1914 amongst those Bokharans who had contact with Russians there were faint though discernable changes in attitudes and assumptions which were to spawn the so-called 'Young Bokhariot' movement after 1918. Khiva was even less affected by its new status. No railway entered its territories and the Imperial government paid little attention to affairs within the khanate. Its government remained in the hands of the traditional elite whose military defeat in 1873 did not affect its internal position, whilst the abolition of slavery apart, its economic and social structure continued intact until 1914. This immobilism was probably reinforced by the military domination which made the region in effect a colony of the Russian army. The governors-general of Turkestan were always serving army officers of the rank of full general, and they were responsible not to the civilian ministries in St Petersburg but to the ministry of war which oversaw all aspects of the governance of the area.  Oblast' and uezd administrations too were headed by serving army officers responsible to the governor-general and wielding both civil and military authority.

The most striking immediate manifestation of the Russian presence was the railway network, whose gradual construction reflected this military predominance.  The earliest schemes for railway development dated from 1873 and were elaborated by de Lesseps in cooperation with N.P. Ignat'ev.  He urged the advantages of an international railway line linking Europe with India and passing through Samarcand.  The proposal caused some ruffled feathers in Britain before sinking without trace.  It may well be however that some similar ideas of linking the Russian and Indian railway systems were entertained by general Annenkov, who was responsible for constructing the Transcaspian Railway.  The genesis of this was to be found in military requirements which in 1880 led to the beginning of what was to become the Transcaspian Railway running eastward from the Caspian Sea firstly to Ashkhabad, then to the Merv oasis and ultimately, via the Amu Darya, to Samarcand, reached in 1888.(22)  A railway link between Samarcand, Tashkent and Andijan begun in 1895 was completed in 1898.  Finally Tashkent was linked to Orenburg and thus to metropolitan Russia by a line begun in 1900 and opened in 1906.  Although these lines were to form the backbone of the region's economic system (the last named being particularily significant) they were military in origin, not civilian, and economic considerations clearly played little part in their planning.  The route of the earliest, transcaspian line lay through the least promising part of the new territories economically speaking, whilst the third was built for strategic reasons on the insistence of the then minister of war, general A.N. Kuropatkin.  Yet by the later 1880s economic development was a reality in the Empire, and all parts of it were being affected to a greater or lesser degree.  A good example of this was the reversal in the relative position of Russian and British goods in the markets of Bokhara.  Whereas in 1883 it had been the latter which had predominated, by 1887 it was the case that

> Bokhara...is replete with the produce of Russian
> manufactories.  The Russian diplomatic agent at
> Bokhara states that English goods are not able to
> compete with Russian products (23)

as Curzon found a year later.  The difference was the result of Russia's ending of the transit trade for foreign goods through the Caucasus via Batum and by the opening of the Transcaspian Railway, which greatly reduced transport costs from European Russia.

Under the impact of these economic developments the 1889 resettlement act removed many of the obstacles to peasant mobility and encouraged movement from the overcrowded interior provinces of European Russia to Siberia and central Asia.  Matters went further in 1896 with the establishment of a resettlement administration positively to encourage such movement and to offer facilities to ease its burdens.  In fact, few Russian peasants reached Turkestan which was already heavily populated, though there was a large influx into the kirgiz and kazhak steppelands provoking considerable trouble between native inhabitants and newcomers. Russian settlement in Turkestan and Transcaspia remained predominantly urban and increased only after 1900 with the growth in the numbers of railway workers and after 1914 with mushrooming military establishments. Anti-settler feeling did develop after the turn of the century and was a significant component in the basmachi movement against the Bolsheviks after 1918. To some extent however it seems to have been a development of traditional anti-city attitudes amongst the rural population. Russian settlement in the khanates of Bokhara and Khiva was small. In Bokhara only in 1887 and 1888 were agreements concluded which permitted Russians to acquire land, and admission to enter was closely controlled by the authorities in Tashkent. By the early 1890s the total Russian resident population stood at about 3,750. In 1910 it had increased to over 20,000, but that included garrisons of Russian troops at Kerki and Termez.

If the resident Russian populations were small, the impact of Russian economic development was nonetheless important for it gradually changed the nature of the local economies and integrated them into the wider Imperial economic system. The changes were however delayed. There were few signs of them during the first quarter century. Indeed, despite the vaunted claims of the importance of central Asia as a cotton-growing area, once the immediate crisis of the mid 1860s arising from the cotton famine of the American Civil War was over there were few attempts to develop or favour central Asian cotton. It was only the attempts first of A.I. Vyshnegradsky and later of S.Yu. Witte to develop and sustain Russia's own industrial base that the cotton resources of central Asia became important. It led to the encouragement of cotton cultivation which in its turn profoundly changed the economic structure of the region.

In 1878 the first duty on raw cotton imports was imposed at a level of 40 kopeks per pud largely in an attempt to raise revenue. It remained unchanged until 1887, when the first Russian protective tariff was introduced. Under it, the duty was raised to 1 rubl in an attempt to increase domestic production in line with the overall objective of fostering home industries. As a result imports of American and Egyptian cotton fell from the high levels of 1886. Simultaneously a major effort was made to persuade central Asian growers to abandon native strains of cotton in favour of the American upland variety with its higher yields and longer staple. The combination led by 1900 to approximately one quarter of the Empire's needs being supplied from central Asia and under the punitive customs duties imposed in 1903 the duty on foreign supplies was quadrupled. By 1914 imported raw cotton accounted for less than half the needs of manufacturing industry and over 11 million puds annually were coming from the region. The chronology strongly suggested that the impelling drive which had brought territorial expansion had not been cotton: the late date of the essential protective tariff and the slow introduction of new varieties suggested that it was not until the Empire required new supplies as a consequence of government-inspired industrial development that the government recognised the value of its new acquisitions. The policies once introduced brought results. In 1886 the area under cotton cultivation in Turkestan had been 13,200 hectares. By 1914 it had increased to 597,200 and the fertile, well-watered districts along the river valleys were areas of monoculture producing raw cotton for the industries of European Russia and importing wheat and other foodstuffs therefrom. The decline in local food production was to have tragic consequences after 1916 when the progressive breakdown in the Russian railway system led to a steep decline in grain flow into Turkestan, resulting in serious famines.

There was also a considerable increase in the area under cotton in both Khiva and Bokhara, though in neither did the same degree of specialisation occur. By 1914 it had increased in Khiva by four times since the early 1880s and the total exceeded fifty-five thousand hectares. Even so this was only about 16% of the total cultivated acreage of the khanate. In Bokhara the 67,775 hectares under cotton in 1913 amounted to no more than 5% of the total cultivated area. These increases in cotton production confirmed that industrial development in Russia made central Asia important as a source of raw cotton for the burgeoning manufacturing industry only during the later 1880s and not at the time of the conquest.

As for trading relationships changes in the pre-conquest position were slow to materialise. Certainly the treaties with Bokhara and Khiva had included clauses advantaging Russian merchants and removing the disabilities under which they operated. The evidence however suggests that they remained dead letters. During the 1870s and early 1880s a steady flow of complaints from Russian merchants claimed that the Bokharan authorities were levying brokerage fees and trade taxes explicitly outlawed by the 1873 Treaty and a similar conclusion was reached in 1908 by Count Pahlen, head of the commission of investigation into the governor-generalship of Turkestan as well as by other Russian officials. The amir of Bokhara, Abd al-Ahad, was actively engaged in the karakaul and cotton-ginning trades and often used his executive power to advance his commercial interests. In this he closely resembled his neighbour, the equally pre-capitalist Abd al-Rahman of Afghanistan. A similar state of affairs reigned in Khiva, where in defiance of the terms of the Treaty of 1873 illegal taxes and impositions were laid on Russian merchants, provoking a steady stream of complaints. There too little improvement had been registered by 1914. If the development of Russian trade had indeed been the driving force behind the military activities of the 1860s and 1870s the Imperial government had not sustained its concern. Only in the area annexed to the Empire was the record more encouraging. Yet in Turkestan too the immediate improvement in the volume of Russian trade was followed by a period of relative stagnation until the later 1880s when a commercial and trading boom set in with the development of cotton cultivation and the spread of a money-based economy.

Central Asia had been acquired by the Russian Empire shortly before the great economic surge of the later nineteenth century began to lift her from the economic sandbank on which she had become stranded at the end of the previous century. Motivated in part by fear for a future in which backward Russian manufacturing industries would be unable to compete with British competition on world markets, the tsarist government had defensively sought to mark out for its subjects an area in which that competition could be minimised and the odds rigged in favour of its own, primitive manufacturing processes. Such defeatism had in fact little chance of success and in the dynamic decades following the Crimean War power within the Empire moved to men whose political creed welcomed economic development for nationalist purposes. In that sense they were true successors to Peter the Great, though some at least of them ostentatiously questioned whether his opening to the West had not been a false step. Nationalists and imperialists, their enthusiasm for modernising the national economy blossomed in the later 1880s whilst their acquisitive activities in central Asia ensured that the impact of economic development was felt there, too.

## Notes

1.  Trans. H. Evans, Russia's Policy in Central Asia 1857-1868 (London, 1964).

2.  P. Lyashchenko, A History of the National Economy of Russia to the 1917 Revolution (New York, 1949).

3.  Cit. N.A. Khalfin, Rossiya i Khanstva Sredney Azii (Moscow, 1974), p.31.

4.  'The Trade of Central Asia', Parl. Papers, xlii, 1864, p.397.

5.  'Report on Russian Trade with Central Asia', Parl. Papers, lxiii, 1862, p.319.

6.  Figures from M.K. Rozhkova, Ekonomicheskie svyazi Rossii so Sredney Azii (Moscow, 1963).

7.  M.N. Pokrovsky, trans.P. von Wahlde, A Brief History of Russia (Orono, Maine, 1968) pp.188-9.

8.  D. Mackenzie, 'Kaufman of Turkestan', Slavic Review 26, 1967, pp.265-285.

9.  Edit. P.A. Zayonchkovsky, Dnevnik Gosudarstvennogo Sekretarya A.A. Polovtsova (2 vols., Moscow, 1966) ii, p.106.

10. F. Kazemzadeh, Russia and Britain in Persia, 1864-1914 (New Haven, 1968), p.416.

11. Edit. H.W. von Schweinitz, Denkwurdigkeiten des Botschafters General H.L. von Schweinitz (2 vols., Berlin, 1927) ii, p.142.

12. H. Rogger, Russia in the Age of Modernisation and Revolution 1881-1917 (London, 1983); E.C. Thaden, Conservative Nationalism in Nineteenth Century Russia (Seattle, 1964); Zayonchkovsky's works are available in translation: The Abolition of Serfdom in Russia (Gulf Breeze, 1978), The Russian Autocracy in Crisis 1878-1882 (Gulf Breeze, 1979), The Russian Autocracy under Alexander III (Gulf Breeze, 1976).

13. A. Walicki, The Slavophile Controversy (Oxford, 1975), p.470.

14. H. Rogger, 'The Skobelev Phenomenon', Oxford Slavonic Papers new series 9, 1976, pp.46-78; O.K. [Olga Novikov], Skobelev and the Slavonic Cause (n.p., 1883).

15. D. Mackenzie, The Lion of Tashkent (Athens, Georgia, 1974).

16. Trans. F.H. Peters, Verestchagin (2 vols., London, 1887).

17. Trans. B. Brasol, The Diary of a Writer (Santa Barbara, 1979), p.1047.

18. L.P. Morris, 'The Subjugation of the Turcomans', Middle Eastern Studies, 15, 1979, pp.193-210.

19. W.B. Lincoln, P.P.Semenov Tian-Shanskii (Newtownville, 1980).

20. D. Rayfield, The Dream of Lhasa (London, 1976).

21. N.A. Khalfin, Rossiya i Bokharskiy Emirat na Zapadnom Pamire (Moscow, 1975).

22. G.N. Curzon, Russia in Central Asia (London, 1889).

23. 'Diplomatic and Consular Report on the Trade of the Consular District of St Petersburg', Parl. Papers, lxxx, 1889, p.155. Compare this with Sir E. Thornton's letter of 9 May 1883 in Parl. Papers, lxxv, 1883, pp.463-4.

# American Expansionism during the Gilded Age, 1865-98

## JOSEPH SMITH

While European powers scrambled for overseas colonies during the last quarter of the nineteenth century, the United States maintained its isolationist and anti-imperialist tradition. The future Democratic presidential candidate, William Jennings Bryan, expressed a characteristically American view when he castigated British imperialism in Egypt as 'mercenary, tyrannical and iniquitous in the extreme and a disgrace to her boasted civilization'. In 1885 president Grover Cleveland in his annual message to Congress underlined the different tradition of American diplomacy

> Maintaining, as I do, the tenets of a line of precedents from Washington's day, which proscribe entangling alliances with foreign states, I do not favor a policy of acquisition of new and distant territory or the incorporation of remote interests with our own.

Such statements reflected the values and ideals of a society that sought deliberately to detach itself from international affairs but yet, at the same time, was conscious of its 'revolutionary' heritage to promote democracy and liberty. Within the western hemisphere American territorial expansion was considerable and the sense of mission knew few limits. 'Today', asserted secretary of state Richard Olney in 1895, 'the United States is practically sovereign on this continent, and its fiat is law upon the subjects to which it confines its interposition.' By 1900 the American eagle had extended its reach beyond the Americas and across the Pacific almost to the shores of China. To contemporaries it appeared that, after decades of diplomatic drift and inertia, the United States had finally come of age and had decided to be an imperialist power. Historical investigation into this subject has proved to be a fruitful field of controversy. The many opinions are so contentious and at variance that a recent scholar has branded this particular academic debate as 'the worst chapter in almost any book'.(1)

## I. The Diplomatic Record, 1865-1900

During the nineteenth century the United States was not usually considered to be a 'great power'. America was geographically distant from Europe, the continent that dominated international events. In general, the United States chose not to be involved in the affairs of the 'Old World', and European nations preferred not to interfere in American matters. Despite its large area and growing population, the American republic lacked the requisite level of military force that conferred the rank of 'great power'. The potential for such status was obviously present and was abundantly demonstrated during the Civil War (1861-65) when the Union mobilised huge armies and created a powerful navy to defeat the attempted secession of the Confederate States. As the Civil War came to its close in 1865, secretary of state William H. Seward confidently used the threat of military intervention to persuade France to abandon its ill-fated scheme to impose a European monarchy upon Mexico. Seward then unveiled an ambitious strategy to acquire various overseas territories in order to strengthen the military security of the United States and also to assist American territorial and commercial expansion. One of Seward's main objectives was the construction of a sea canal through the isthmus of Central America. To implement this goal required not only a treaty with Colombia, in whose territory the canal would be located, but in addition led Seward to propose the further acquisition of a chain of island bases ranging from the Dominican Republic and Cuba in the Caribbean to Hawaii and Midway in the Pacific.

'Comprehensive national policy', declared president Andrew Johnson to Congress in 1868, 'would seem to sanction the acquisition and incorporation into our Federal Union of the several adjacent and insular communities.' Congress was not persuaded and would only approve one purchase, that of Alaska from Russia in 1867. Despite the derisory references in the press of 'Seward's Folly' and 'Seward's Icebox', Congress regarded Russia's desire to sell as an opportunity similar to Jefferson's Louisiana Purchase of 1803. The acquisition of territory non-contiguous to the United States represented a departure from American tradition, but Seward could claim few other diplomatic successes. Indeed, the post-Civil War years are regarded as a period of 'anti-expansionism'. The military might of the Union was rapidly demobilised. A tiny standing army was retained primarily for garrison duty and Indian fighting. By 1890 its size was no more than 28,000 men which placed it about thirteenth in the world, behind countries such as Belgium and Bulgaria. The navy was also allowed to fall into decay, so much so that it was described as late as 1885 as 'an alphabet of floating washtubs'. Military decline reflected and mirrored domestic attitudes. American society was complacent and provincial. Its attention and energies were absorbed by the challenge of peopling the vast north American continent and building up the economy. Politics were dominated by narrowly-defined partisan issues such as reconstruction and later in the 1880s and 1890s by civil service reform, the currency and interminable congressional debates over the tariff. There was little public enthusiasm or even interest in ambitious schemes for territorial expansion. In the words of Henry Adams, Seward 'went somewhat too far and too fast for the public'.

The preoccupation with internal affairs was reflected in the size and status of the American diplomatic establishment. The two decades following the Civil War have in fact been described as the 'nadir' of American diplomacy. Democratic tradition combined with congressional indifference and parsimony to resist both the concept of and the need for a professional foreign service fashioned on European aristocratic lines. 'It is a well-known fact', alleged William E. Curtis in 1899, 'that the diplomatic service of the United States is small in numbers and receives less compensation than that of any other of the great nations of the world.' Nevertheless, each new presidential administration was inundated with pleas and entreaties for diplomatic and consular office. Four hundred men a day personally waited upon Hamilton Fish for this purpose during his first few weeks as secretary of state in 1869. Prevailing political considerations rather than particular qualifications or merit dictated the selection of officials. Not surprisingly, all too many of those appointed incurred criticism rather than respect for America when they came to take up their posts abroad.

Unhappily, scandal was not confined to the diplomatic service. This was the period of the 'gilded' age in which American politics became a byword for maladministration and corruption. A series of financial scandals clouded the presidential years of Ulysses S. Grant (1869–77). Congressional suspicion of the administration's economic self-interest compelled Grant to abandon his attempt to purchase the Caribbean island of the Dominican Republic in 1870. The cautious diplomacy of secretary of state Hamilton Fish towards the long rebellion against Spanish rule in Cuba (1868–78) was further evidence of a disposition to avoid becoming directly involved in foreign affairs.

Diplomatic initiatives were rare during the Grant administrations. Nevertheless, Fish did show a close concern over events in Cuba and he also demonstrated an interest in Nicaragua as a possible new site for a central American canal. Furthermore, a trade treaty was concluded with Hawaii in 1875. The agreement allowed the American navy to use Pearl Harbor as a naval base and underlined the close economic relationship that was emerging between America and Hawaii. The succeeding administration of president Rutherford B. Hayes (1877–1881) was committed to the politics of the 'dead centre' and showed no great interest in foreign affairs. In 1879–80, however, the efforts of the French entrepreneur, Ferdinand de Lesseps, to raise capital to begin construction of an isthmian canal provoked hostile comment in the United States. The administration responded to public alarm but with words and not deeds. 'The policy of this country', Hayes told Congress, 'is a canal under American control.' De Lesseps was not deterred and his company soon began work on the projected canal.

The brief presidency of James A. Garfield began in March 1881. His secretary of state, James G. Blaine, launched a spirited and controversial Latin American policy that would later earn him the nickname of 'Jingo Jim'. Blaine condemned European meddling in the New World. His aim was to extend American political and economic influence over Latin America. This attitude almost involved the United States in the War of the Pacific between Chile, Peru and Bolivia (1879–84). Blaine's period in office was, however, cut short by Garfield's assassination in the summer of 1881. The secretary of state was compelled to resign, but before leaving office he proposed a meeting of all the American republics ostensibly to resolve all outstanding hemispheric disputes. The conference would be held in Washington in order to demonstrate American leadership.

Blaine's dramatic and unsolicited invitations were withdrawn by his successor, although the new administration of Chester A. Arthur (1881-85) pursued a policy towards Latin America that was not all that dissimilar from that of Blaine. In 1884 secretary of state Frederick Frelinghuysen justified the sending of a trade commission to Latin America

> I am thoroughly convinced of the advisability of knitting closely our relations with the states of this continent, and no effort on my part shall be wanting to accomplish a result so consonant with the constant policy of this country, and in the spirit of the Monroe doctrine, which, in excluding foreign political interference, recognizes the common interest of the states of North and South America.

The administration busied itself investigating canal schemes and negotiating trade treaties with various Latin American countries, but there was little practical result. The Buenos Aires Herald expressed a common criticism in November 1885

> During the last few years we have heard a great amount of talk about the encouragement of closer commercial relations between the United States and the countries of South America. Papers have printed tons of paper about this matter. Congress has created commissions, who have gone junketing about the world with no end of fur and feathers, making a loud noise – and doing nothing...
>
> So long as Europe comes here with its millions and Americans come here with itinerating commissions, the business supremacy of Europe in this country will be seen.

During the 1880s American diplomacy was also showing an interest beyond the western hemisphere and, for example, the Arthur administration established relations with Korea in 1882. An awareness of African affairs was demonstrated by the sending of an American delegation to the Berlin conference (1884-85). The first administration of Grover Cleveland (1885-89) showed a concern for the future of Samoa in the Pacific. Under president Benjamin Harrison (1889-93) the United States agreed to participate in a joint Anglo-American-German protectorate over the islands. This latter development also indicated the growing naval power of the United States. In 1883 Congress voted the first of a series of appropriations to modernise the American navy by building up-to-date steel cruisers. Three years later an order was placed for the first of a number of battleships. By the end of the century the American navy was regarded as the third most powerful in the world.

The primary emphasis of American foreign policy, however, remained on western hemispheric affairs and this was symbolised by the holding of the Pan-American conference in Washington (1889-90). William E. Curtis noted that 1889 marked the centennial of the American Constitution and that it was fitting that the 'mother of republics' should celebrate the occasion 'by bringing her children together'. The conference achieved little, but the very fact that it had taken place was a recognition of the rising power and influence of the United States within the hemisphere. The Harrison administration followed up the conference by concluding a number of reciprocal trade agreements with Latin American countries. Moreover, during the 1890s a series of events occurred in Latin America that prompted a vigorous American diplomatic response. An attack by a mob upon American sailors on shore leave in Valparaiso in 1891 resulted in the dispatch of warships to Chile and the issue of an uncompromising ultimatum by Harrison to that government. American warships also influenced the course of events in Brazil in 1893-94 and Nicaragua in 1894. The overthrow of the Hawaiian monarchy in 1893 presented an opportunity for the annexation of the islands. The incoming Cleveland administration (1893-97), however, rejected annexation. 'I am unalterably opposed', declared secretary of state Walter Q. Gresham in 1894, 'to stealing territory, or of annexing a people against their consent, and the people of Hawaii do not favor annexation.'

By contrast, the administration judged that the people of Venezuela required American assistance in their boundary dispute with Britain. Lobbyists employed by the Venezuelan government convinced Cleveland that Britain was intriguing to seize territory in violation of the Monroe doctrine. The President feared that should Britain succeed

> there is nothing to prevent her taking the whole
> of Venezuela or any other South American state.
> If Great Britain can do this with impunity,
> France and Germany will do it also.

An Anglo-American crisis erupted in 1895 when the United States demanded that the dispute go to arbitration. After initial hesitation, a diplomatically isolated British government gave way to American pressure and agreed to arbitration.

In February 1895 a new struggle against Spanish rule had broken out in Cuba. The war was conducted with savagery and brutality on both sides, although the American press and public were quick to sympathise with the rebels in their fight for liberty from a tyrannical imperial ruler. President Cleveland and his successor, William McKinley (president from 1897 to 1901), resisted public pressure for American military intervention. Both men wished to avoid war and sought to use the influence of the United States to bring about the speedy peaceful settlement between the Spanish government and the rebels. Pacification proved to be constantly elusive and by the beginning of 1898 the policy of mediation had collapsed. The continued atrocities of the civil war, the unexplained blowing up of the American battleship _Maine_ while on a courtesy visit to Havana and McKinley's realisation that Spanish promises to introduce reforms in Cuba had no foundation, brought the United States to war with Spain in April 1898. The decision for armed intervention was regarded as an honourable act, prompted by humanitarian motives and designed to liberate the Cuban people. This was underlined by the Senate's adoption of an amendment prepared by senator Henry Teller of Colorado disclaiming any American intention to annex Cuba and declaring that America's purpose was 'to leave the government and control of the island to its people'.

The Spanish-American war was, however, not solely confined to the Caribbean. Spain also possessed colonies and military resources in the Pacific. Consequently, while American troops were preparing to invade Cuba, the American Pacific squadron under commodore George Dewey was ordered to destroy Spanish naval forces in the Pacific. On 1 May 1898 Dewey attacked and destroyed the Spanish fleet at Manila Bay. A political vacuum was created in the Philippine Islands and Dewey assumed administrative control. Military reinforcements were dispatched from the United States to consolidate American possession of the islands. In Cuba the 'splendid little war' soon ended in Spanish defeat, but the peace settlement was concerned not so much with the future of Cuba than with the unexpected question of what the United States should do with the Philippines. In accordance with the Teller amendment, the people of Cuba were to be given their independence. But there was no such constitutional guidance in the matter of the Philippines. A public debate ensued between advocates of 'imperialism' and 'anti-imperialism'. Both sides marshalled impressive arguments and the debate cut across party political lines. President McKinley decided in favour of annexation of the Philippines and a treaty to this effect was narrowly ratified by the Senate in February 1899.

Other overseas territory also came under American control. In the Caribbean the small Spanish island of Puerto Rico was taken as a war indemnity and to remove Spanish rule from the Americas. In August 1898 the need to supply and reinforce the new American military presence in the Philippines had resulted in the annexation of the Hawaiian Islands. The islands of Guam and Wake were also occupied so that by 1899 the United States possessed a chain of islands stretching across the Pacific.

Nor did the expansionism stop with the Philippines. Public interest in Asia had been aroused by Dewey's victory at Manila Bay and by the debate over imperialism. In 1899 and 1900 secretary of state John Hay issued his 'open door' notes to assert the emerging American political and economic interest in China. In August 1900 five thousand American troops were sent to Peking to combat the Boxer rising. After decades of apparently aimless diplomacy, it seemed that the United States had become a world power with a world role within a short space of time. Despite the closeness of the vote over annexation, Americans had rejected the anti-imperialist tradition in favour of taking up 'the

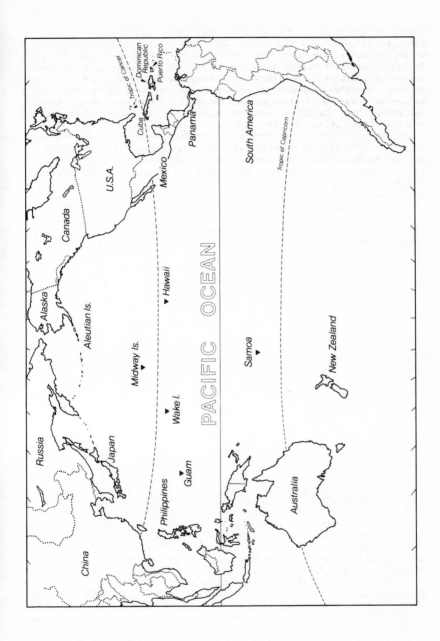

Islands and Regions principally affected by US Expansionism

white man's burden'. McKinley envisaged the future of the Philippines as

> a land of plenty and of increasing possibilities;
> a people redeemed from savage and indolent
> habits, devoted to the arts of peace, in touch
> with the commerce and trade of all nations,
> enjoying the blessing of freedom, of civil and
> religious liberty, of education, and of homes,
> and whose children and children's children shall
> for ages hence bless the American republic
> because it emancipated their fatherland, and set
> them in the pathway of the world's best
> civilization.

The actual course of events was, however, not so ideal. Empire reaffirmed and stimulated the American sense of national pride and mission, but the outbreak of rebellion in the Philippines and political disorder in Cuba underscored the complications and burdens of being an imperial power.

## II. The Historical Debate

### 1. Imperialism

'Imperialism' is a word that has undesirable connotations so that its use has been resisted as a description of American diplomacy. A recent writer has noted the frequent disavowal by American presidents of the desire for territory 'in order to demonstrate their own and the nation's freedom from the sin of imperialism'.(2) Indeed McKinley spoke of the United States as becoming a 'world power'. He avoided the words 'empire' and 'colonies' and preferred to explain his policy as being guided by the dictates of duty and humanitarianism.

Many modern historians, however, openly adopt the term 'imperialism'. Ernest May has called his book, American Imperialism while a widely used textbook by Gardner, LaFeber and McCormick has the title, Creation of the American Empire. Moreover, in the debate of 1898-99 mention of 'imperialism' could hardly be avoided because the opponents of annexation formally called themselves the 'Anti-Imperialist League'. The League did not condemn 'expansionism'. The republic had a long history of territorial acquisitions by means of settlement, purchase and war, but these lands had been taken with the intention that they would be ultimately admitted as states of the Union. Hawaii and the Philippines were different and the anti-imperialists argued that their annexation would be a departure from American tradition. 'If we adopt the policy of acquiring tropical countries, where republics cannot live', warned senator Pettigrew of South Dakota during the debate on the annexation of Hawaii, 'we overturn the theory upon which this Government is established.' A similar argument had defeated Grant's attempt to purchase the Dominican Republic in 1870. The contest was, however, much closer in 1898-99. Politicans approached the question cautiously. A typical attitude was expressed by senator Penrose of Pennsylvania in June 1898

> Neither in our suddenly acquired position in the affairs of the world nor in our desire for trade extension is there as yet, and I hope there never will be, any sentiment among our people for mere territorial acquisition; but there is a well-defined sentiment...that the United States should acquire such territory, like the islands of Hawaii, as is absolutely necessary...for the better protection of the American continent from foreign aggression and for the promotion and extension of our foreign commerce.

Neither expansionist senators not the McKinley administration proposed unlimited territorial expansion. Rather than a positive striving for empire it seemed that new responsibilities and duties were being thrust upon America. A topic of genuine concern was the future of the people of the Philippines. If the United States withdrew from the Islands, would the Filipinos subsequently fall under the sway of British or German imperialism? By contrast, annexation by the United States would serve a humanitarian and not an exploitative purpose. President McKinley declared that American rule would seek 'to educate the Filipinos, and uplift and Christianize them'. America was not pursuing selfish and aggressive policies and was only acquiring relatively small areas of land. There was no intention of imitating the imperialism practised by the despised nations of the 'Old World'.

Throughout the late nineteenth century there had been little support in Congress and amongst American public opinion for the acquisition of overseas territory. In 1898 the Teller amendment affirmed this by proclaiming that the United States had neither the disposition nor intention 'to exercize sovereignty, jurisdiction, or control' over Cuba. Within a year, however, Congress had approved the annexation of Hawaii and the Philippines. The decision was reached only after a lengthy and impressive public debate on the issue. Not surprisingly the vote in the Senate was extremely close - a bare two-thirds majority plus one vote in favour of the annexation of the Philippines. Consequently, American power and prestige became bound up with the exercise of control over distant lands and alien peoples. The diplomatic historian, Samuel F. Bemis, could only explain this sudden and uncharacteristic turn of events as a 'great aberration'. By its demonstration of armed might and assertion of moral superiority over allegedly 'inferior' peoples, the United States pursued a diplomacy not markedly different from that of the European powers. Whether such a policy is described as 'imperialist', 'colonialist' or 'expansionist' is merely a semantic issue. 'For better or for worse', concluded the distinguished Harvard professor, Archibald C. Coolidge, in 1908, 'the United States has thus become a colonial power in the fullest sense of the word.'

## 2. Continuity versus Discontinuity

Historical controversy has also surrounded the question whether the decision to acquire an overseas empire in 1898-99 marked a

new departure in American foreign policy or whether it represented the
culmination of preceding events dating from the expansionism of the
Civil War period or even going as far back as the birth of the republic.
The contemporary debate was absorbed by the immediacy of events and
stressed the element of discontinuity rather than continuity with the
past.   So unexpected and wonderful were the American victories at sea
and on land that McKinley saw the hand of God at work.   In a celebrated
interview the president recalled how he agonised over what to do with
the Philippines and how the truth was eventually revealed to him

> I walked the floor of the White House night after
> night until midnight; and I am not ashamed to
> tell you, gentlemen, that I went down on my knees
> and prayed Almighty God for light and guidance
> more than one night.   And one night late it came
> to me this way - I don't know how it was, but it
> came.

According to this statement empire had been thrust upon the United
States.   The fact that Dewey's victory at Manila Bay came out of the
blue and had astounded a delighted public confirmed the element of
chance.   'Our navy', noted one writer in Atlantic magazine, 'has
revealed to ourselves not less than to the rest of the world our
rightful place among the nations.'   From being something perceived as
rather  alien  and  disreputable  empire  now  became  acceptable.
Missionaries who had once condemned or had been indifferent to
imperialism now viewed annexation as the answer to the humanitarian
dilemma of how to help the Filipinos.   The military victory over Spain
also created new strategic imperatives and commercial opportunities.
Thus, Julius Pratt has shown how businessmen who were opposed to
territorial expansion in the early months of 1898 had dramatically
altered their opinions by the end of the year.

Frederick Merk has also concentrated his attention on 1898
and has attached singular importance to one particular event.   In his
opinion, the blowing up of the U.S. battleship Maine in February 1898
while on a courtesy visit to Havana harbour, was an event of unique
significance

> It is a truism of political science that an
> incident of startling character occurring during
> an international controversy in which popular
> emotions have become deeply engaged, has an
> impact abnormally great on the public mind.
> Especially is this true if the incident has
> involved the shedding of American blood on
> American soil or on an American vessel innocently
> employed abroad.   In such a case the public mind
> is stormed, reason departs, emotion takes over,
> and extremism, which is latent in every society,
> emerges and takes command.(3)

If the Maine has not been destroyed, would the Spanish-American war have
occurred in 1898?   If there had not been a Spanish-American war, would
the United States still have become an imperialist power?   The accident
theory of history is an entertaining game to play and the speculation

can go on indefinitely. Although the interpretation stressing discontinuity with the past has been widely held by American historians, few recent scholars are inclined to place so much significance on a particular incident or year in the past. In their attempts to understand and to explain why things happened, these writers usually discern a continuity or pattern of events. Richard Van Alstyne, for example, emphasises the inherently expansionist nature of American history and regards the words 'empire-building', 'imperialism', 'manifest destiny', and 'expansionism' as interchangeable

> the United States is a national ·state, so conceived and so dedicated by its eighteenth century founders, and as such it possesses the attributes and the drives which have made it in fact a typically ambitious and expanding national state. In its energies, which never seem to slacken, and in its thrusts outward, it is the Germany of the American continents.(4)

Territorial expansion in the shape of the expanding frontier was intrinsic to the American experience of the nineteenth century. Expansion was particularly extensive and dynamic during the period of 'manifest destiny' of the 1840s and it has been argued that this was also the motivating force of the 1890s. The legacy of the expansionist tradition was undoubtedly present at the end of the century, but the links are somewhat tenuous in that 'manifest destiny' was a continental phenomenon occurring at a particular time. Professor Merk concludes

> The imperialism of the 1890's is regarded by some historians as a variant merely of Manifest Destiny of the 1840's. This is an error. It was the antithesis of Manifest Destiny. Manifest Destiny was continentalism. It meant absorption of North America.... Expansionism in 1899 was insular and imperialistic. Its inspiration was nationalism of a sort. It involved the reduction of distant peoples to a state of colonialism.(5)

Another interpretation seeks to establish a continuity of events between the 1890s and the post Civil War expansionist policies of William H. Seward. Certainly, the territorial and commercial ambitions of Seward possessed many similarities to those of the 'imperialists' at the close of the century, but, with the exception of the purchase of Alaska, Seward's schemes were invariably rejected by Congress and public opinion. Rather than being a direct precursor of future generations of 'imperialists', Seward might be seen as the last of the generation of expansionists dating from the years of 'manifest destiny' and antebellum America.

The drab years of diplomacy that followed Seward's expansionism, however, gave way to the 'spirited' policies of the 1880s. Robert Beisner perceives the decade of the 1880s as a historical watershed separating the 'old' from the 'new' diplomacy. It was a time when the whole of society was experiencing substantial economic, social and demographic change and this was reflected in the conduct of and the new importance attached to foreign affairs. 'A new era in American

AACA-G

diplomatic history opened sometime around 1890', argues Beisner, 'and the policymaker of 1895 differed sharply from his 1885 predecessor.'(6) A number of historians broadly share Beisner's view and also concentrate their research and writings on the last decade and a half of the ninteenth century. These scholars also stress the coincidence of economic and social crisis of these years, but their interpretations differ according to how much weight they give to particular ideological or economic factors.


## 3. Ideological Imperialism

During the 1880s and 1890s American society displayed a growing awareness that the United States was fast becoming a world power with an international role. The former secretary of state, Richard Olney, wrote in May 1898 that the United States ought

> to recognize the changed conditions and to realize its great place among the powers of the earth. It behoves it to accept the commanding position belonging to it, with all its advantages on the one hand and all its burdens on the other. It is not enough for it to vaunt its greatness and superiority and to call upon the rest of the world to admire and be duly impressed. The mission of this country...is not merely to pose but to act – and, while always governing itself by the rule of prudence and common sense and making its own special interests the first and paramount objects of its care, to forego no fitting opportunity to further the progress of civilization.

Olney's positive analysis was repeated in many contemporary speeches, books and articles. The historian, John Fiske, popularised Darwin's theory of evolution and asserted that the anglo-saxons had proved themselves the 'fittest' of all the races. In a frequently quoted passage from his book, Our Country, the Congregational clergyman, Josiah Strong, predicted

> If I read not amiss, this powerful race will move down upon Mexico, down upon Central and South America, out upon the islands of the sea, over upon Africa and beyond. And can any one doubt that the result of this competition will be the 'survival of the fittest'?

A similar theme was expressed by the geopolitician and philosopher, Brooks Adams, whose Law of Civilization and Decay urged the historical inevitability of overseas expansion. This cyclical view of history found a receptive and admiring audience amongst several of the leading politicians of the day.

Another historical interpretation stressed strategic imperatives even more precisely. Admiral Alfred T. Mahan, author of The Influence of Sea Power Upon History, argued that national greatness

depended upon naval power. He bemoaned America's lack of a modern navy,
a strong merchant marine and adequate coastal defences. For many years
he advocated a powerful battleship navy with commensurate world-wide
naval bases. More for party political and commercial rather than for
strategic reasons, Congress had voted for appropriations to build up the
navy so that by the 1890s an impressive 'new' navy was in existence.
Nonetheless, the possession of military power combined with the
increasing consciousness of social darwinism and anglo-saxonism to
facilitate and prompt a more active American role in world affairs.
Senator Henry Cabot Lodge of Massachusetts coined the phrase 'the large
policy' and urged its implementation upon the McKinley administration.
Julius Pratt summed up Lodge's aim as seeking to make the United States

> the indisputable dominant power in the western
> hemisphere, possessed of a great navy, owning and
> controlling an Isthmian canal, holding naval
> bases in the Caribbean and the Pacific, and
> contesting, on at least even terms with the
> greatest powers, the naval and commercial
> supremacy of the Pacific Ocean and the Far
> East.(7)

Even as early as 1895 the navy department had prepared contingency plans
for an attack on the Philippines. The assertive ideology of the 1880s
and 1890s was preparing and propelling America into an imperial power.
The presence of Dewey's squadron in the Pacific, his attack upon Manila
Bay and the annexation of the Philippines should not therefore be
regarded as totally unexpected and inexplicable.

Anglo-saxon racism was growing in popularity during the
1890s, but it was not a new phenomenon in American society and had
existed earlier in the century without leading to imperialist
consequences. James Field has cogently queried the extent of the
influence of ideological imperialism. He argues that Fiske and Strong
were not widely read by the public and that their speeches and writings
were almost wholly preoccupied with domestic rather than foreign
affairs. Field makes the point that Brooks Adams did not publish
anything specifically on foreign policy until the summer of 1898. He
also contends that Mahan has been misunderstood and that the admiral
never advocated an imperialist programme. 'But navies can be designed
for various purposes', remarks Field, 'there is no necessary connection
between naval building and commercial expansion or colonization, and
battleships do not equate with empire.'

Furthermore, it is debatable as to how influential were the
advocates of 'the large policy'. Lodge was a distinguished senator, but
he was not a member of McKinley's inner circle. The most celebrated
'imperialist', Theodore Roosevelt, served in the relatively minor office
of assistant secretary of the navy. McKinley has been pictured as a
weak and ineffectual leader, easily swayed and manipulated by
expansionists and the 'yellow' press, but modern biographers have
refuted this interpretation. 'We now recognize', comments Beisner,
'that he was a resourceful political leader and minor master in managing
those around him.'(8)

Expansionist ideas were undeniably present in the 1890s, but their impact upon the shaping of events is difficult, if not impossible to evaluate. A more tangible line of investigation emphasises the significance of economic factors.

## 4. Economic Imperialism

The economic interpretation of American foreign policy owes most to the works of William A. Williams and especially to The Tragedy of American Diplomacy, which was first published in 1959. So considerable has been Williams' influence that he has inspired the creation of a 'Wisconsin school' of diplomatic historians. Williams sees the need and the desire to extend the marketplace for American agricultural goods as the dynamic force of much of American history. American society has shown this by demonstrating 'the firm conviction, even dogmatic belief, that America's domestic well-being depends upon such sustained, ever-increasing overseas economic expansion'.(9)    The debate, therefore, focuses not on whether Americans wished to become an empire but on how this was achieved. Until the late nineteenth century 'empire' was achieved within continental limits or by the gradual spread of 'informal empire' over the western hemisphere and islands of the Pacific.    The transformation of America from an agricultural to an industrial economy, however, both accelerated and altered this development towards the close of the nineteenth century.    This particular period has consequently been given special significance by the Wisconsin school.    Walter LaFeber uses the term 'the new empire'. He stresses the growing public anxiety over the problem of agricultural overproduction in the late-1870s and how this mood was aggravated by a series of economic crises in the mid-1880s culminating in the 'great depression' of 1893-97.    'There is no sufficient market for our surplus agricultural products except a foreign market', noted the economist, David A. Wells, in 1884.    Coincidentally, manufacturers and industrialists were also coming to the fore in society and politics and they, too, were seeking overseas outlets for their goods and capital. Diplomats responded to this domestic pressure by 'depression diplomacy' in which they directed their efforts towards promoting American exports. Latin America and especially China were regarded as particularly promising markets.    A rather flowery but not untypical example of business sentiment was contained in the American Exporter of May 1881

> No greater field for commercial enterprise can be found than that offered in the vast and undeveloped markets of China for our manufacturers and farmers.... Its vast rivers and canals present unrivalled scope for our steam navigation, and its wide plains and valleys offer matchless facilities for railways.... It stands upon the threshold of the New World and offers to America the greater share of a trade which has enriched every community which has been able to command it.(10)

Dewey's victory at Manila Bay fulfilled the hopes and calculations of the economic expansionists by directing public attention to the Pacific.    The Philippines were valued not so much for humanitarian or strategic reasons, but because they provided access to the fabled 'China market'. The 'open door' notes presented by secretary of state Hay in 1899 and 1900 underlined the significance of China. William A. Williams believes that historians have misunderstood the importance of Hay's actions

> They missed its deep roots in the American past
> and its importance at the time, and they failed
> to realize that the policy expressed the basic
> strategy and tactics of America's secular and
> imperial expansion in the twentieth century.
> When combined with the ideology of an industrial
> Manifest Destiny, the history of the Open Door
> Notes became the history of American foreign
> relations from 1900 to 1958.(11)

The economic interpretation has had particular appeal to those writers and readers already holding a critical view of the excessive and corrupting influence of capitalism upon recent American foreign policy. American diplomacy has been influenced by business interests, but this does not prove the existence of a systematic and consistent policy designed to promote American economic penetration throughout the world. Despite the rhetoric of expansionists, no such policy was apparent in the late nineteenth century. Political debate tended to be dominated by narrow and partisan considerations. Improved trading relations with foreign countries were frequently sacrificed in the domestic political battle over the protective tariff. The attempts to encourage overseas trade by means of reciprocity treaties were uniformly treated by Congress with suspicion. Moreover, congressional parsimony towards the merchant marine and the foreign service underlined the prevailing provincial, anti-expansionist attitude.

In the age of _laisser faire_ businessmen did not always seek or expect government assistance or intervention in their affairs. The pattern of American exports remained fairly consistent throughout the nineteenth century. The most important purchasers remained Europe and Canada. During the last quarter of the century Latin America and Asia imported on average no more than one-seventh of total American exports. Moreover, American businessmen remained preoccupied with their own home market. In 1870 secretary of state Fish deplored the fact that Latin Americans bought twice as much from Britain as they did from the United States. Despite the efforts of expansionists, twenty-five years later a congressional report still lamented the small share that Americans possesed of the Latin American import trade. During the 1880s and 1890s there was evidence of increasing American interest in Asia, but this was also tempered by growing nativist hostility to oriental immigration into the states of the west coast. 'Most Americans lacked any real conviction of the importance of the Far East', comments David Pletcher and he considers that the United States pursued a 'hesitant' policy towards that region. 'It is therefore highly misleading', concludes Robert Beisner, 'to think in terms of a unified American business community, backed by a determined government, striving unremittingly to break into the markets of Asia and Latin America.'(12)

## 5. Psychological Imperialism

A famous article by Richard Hofstadter described the 1890s as a time of 'psychic crisis' for American society.(13)   Anxiety over the increasing influx of 'new' immigrants from the Mediterranean countries and eastern Europe, the mounting evidence of the baneful effects of industrialisation, the political corruption and social evils associated with the mushrooming cities, the 'closing of the frontier', coincided with severe economic depression to create an atmosphere of pervasive gloom and disorder.   As an army of unemployed and discontented men prepared to march on Washington in 1894, secretary of state Gresham spoke alarmingly of the 'symptoms of revolution'.   According to Hofstadter, Americans sought relief and escape from this psychic crisis by directing their thoughts and energies into domestic political reform movements and also into external outlets such as imperial expansion. The doubting and questioning of values and beliefs extended to the anti-imperialist tradition especially since empire offered a number of attractions.   It alleviated insecurity by reinforcing the concept of the superiority of the anglo-saxon race.   War and the annexation of distant territory also allowed the expression of aggressive impulses while at the same time appearing as an idealistic and humanitarian crusade.

The 1890s were indeed dark years for the republic, but since that time American society has experienced similar difficult periods of demographic change, social disturbance and an even more severe economic depression during the 1930s without there being any irresistible public demand for an aggressive foreign policy.   Like the assessment of the influence of ideas, any correlation between psychological insecurity and diplomacy is notoriously difficult to substantiate.   Hofstadter has focused attention on the domestic turmoil of the 1890s, but the case of 'psychic crisis' as the cause of imperialism is tenuous and circumstantial.

## 6. Conclusion

That the United States annexed distant overseas territories in 1898-99 is historical fact.   Whether this was an example of formal or informal imperialism, colonialism or expansionism is a matter of historical debate.   Scholars have put forward various interpretations and each is not without merit.   Events of momentous significance did occur in 1898, but to understand them fully the historian must investigate their background.   But how far back into the past should he go?   Whatever watershed or transitional point is selected, there will inevitably be a subjective emphasis upon particular facts at the expense of passing over others.   In general, most writers prefer to concentrate on the 1880s and 1890s.   During these years the United States became a nation of continental extent, a leading industrial economy and a naval power of the first rank.   The result was a growing national consciousness and self-assertiveness.   'The old nations of the earth creep on at a snail's pace', declared the iron and steel millionaire, Andrew Carnegie, and he exulted that 'the Republic thunders past with the rush of an express'.   An inherent economic dynamism made more urgent by the incidence of overproduction and severe depression directed attention beyond the borders of the United States.   In addition, world events frequently called for an American response.   The age of imperialism and realignment of alliances presented diplomatic dangers and opportunities. American diplomats were especially vigilant over developments in Latin America and took advantage of European weaknesses to assert American political preeminence in the western hemisphere. The victory over Spain in 1898 presented the unexpected quandary of what to do with the Philippines. Annexation appealed to material self-interest. While it might be condemned as a violation of American values and traditions, it could also be interpreted as a chance to fulfil America's idealistic sense of mission to promote democracy and civilisation. The cautious McKinley chose in favour of acquiring empire and his recommendation was narrowly approved by the Senate. The United States had therefore decided to become actively involved in world affairs. Expanding American power had interacted with international politics and the result was American 'imperialism'.

# Notes

1. J.A. Field, 'American Imperialism: the worst chapter in almost any book', American Historical Review, 83, 1978, pp.644-683.

2. R. Zevin, 'An Interpretation of American Imperialism', Journal of Economic History, 32, 1972, pp.316-360.

3. F. Merk, Manifest Destiny and Mission in American History (New York, 1963), p.248.

4. R. van Alstyne, The American Empire (Historical Association Pamphlet no. G.43, London, 1960).

5. Merk, op.cit., pp.256-7.

6. R.L. Beisner, From the Old Diplomacy to the New 1865-1900, (New York, 1975), p.66.

7. J.W. Pratt, 'The "Large Policy" of 1898', Mississippi Valley Historical Review, 19, 1932.

8. Beisner, op.cit., p.109.

9. W.A. Williams, The Tragedy of American Diplomacy (Cleveland, 1962), p.11.

10. Cit. in D.M. Pletcher, 'Rhetoric and Results: a Pragmatic View of American Economic Expansion, 1865-1898', Diplomatic History, 5, 1981, p.94.

11. Williams, op.cit., p.45.

12. Beisner, op.cit., p.22.

13. 'Cuba, the Philippines and Manifest Destiny' in R. Hofstadter, The Paranoid Style in American Politics (New York, 1966).

# BIBLIOGRAPHICAL NOTES

## General and Introductory

In addition to the works mentioned in the footnotes the following is a small selection from the enormous literature available. As a brief introduction there is M.E. Chamberlain, The New Imperialism (Historical Association pamphlet G.73, London, 1970) whilst the differing interpretations of imperialism are summarised in T. Kemp, Theories of Imperialism (London, 1971) and A.P. Thornton, Doctrines of Imperialism (New York, 1965). D.K. Fieldhouse's Theory of Capitalist Imperialism (London, 1967) is a useful collection of texts, whilst his Economics and Empire, 1830-1914 (London, 1973) is an exhaustive survey. A recent re-examination of the whole period from 1815 until 1960 from a radical perspective is V.G. Kiernan, European Empires from Conquest to Collapse, 1815-1960 (London, 1982). All these works offer extensive guidance to further reading. A useful selection of passages illustrating nineteenth-century thinking on the colonial relationship is edit. P.D. Curtin, Imperialism (London, 1971).

On the specifically economic aspects an excellent general guide to original contributions, both marxist and non-marxist, and to recent assessments of their work is edit. R. Owen and B. Sutcliffe, Studies in the Theory of Imperialism (London, 1972) which contains a helpful, annotated bibliography. Offering different perspectives are M. Barratt-Brown, The Economics of Imperialism (London, 1974) and A. Hodgart, The Economics of European Imperialism (London, 1977). New currents in the marxist approach may be observed in E. Laclau, Politics and Ideology in Marxist Theory (London, 1977). Most recent departures in the general debate are explored in S. Amin, Unequal development (London, 1976); A. Emmanuel, Unequal Exchange (New York, 1972); and I. Wallerstein, The Capitalist World Economy (Cambridge, 1979).

For individual countries not covered by the separate bibliographies below the following may be consulted. For Britain the best survey is B. Porter, The Lion's Share (London, 1975) which contains a good guide to the available literature. M.E. Chamberlain's Origins of Modern German Colonialism (New York, 1921) and The Rise and Fall of Germany's Colonial Empire, 1884-1918 (New York, 1930) may be supplemented by H. Pogge von Strandmann, 'Domestic origins of Germany's colonial expansion under Bismarck', Past and Present, 42, 1969, pp.140-159 and H.U. Wehler, 'Bismarck's Imperialism, 1862-1890', ibid., 48, 1970, pp.119-155. On France in addition to H. Brunschwig's major work French Colonialism 1871-1914 (London, 1966) there are recent studies by C.M. Andrews and A.S. Kanya-Forstner, 'The French Colonial Party: its Composition, Aims and Influence, 1885-1914', Historical Journal, 14, 1971, pp.99-128 and their France Overseas: the Great War and the climax of French Imperial Expansion (London, 1981), especially the first two chapters.

# Latin America from Indepence to Dependence

General approaches to economic aspects of imperialism include the works cited above by Owen and Sutcliffe, Barratt-Brown, Hodgart, Laclau, Amin and Emmanuel. These may be supplemented by the Latin American flavour of A. Cueva, El desarrollo del capitalismo en América Latina (Mexico, 1978).

There have been a number of successful attempts to school the dependency debate over Latin America. Among the best are J.G. Palma, 'Dependency, a formal theory of underdevelopment or a methodology for the analysis of concrete situations of underdevelopment?', in World Development VI (1978), and several contributions by Philip J. O'Brien. O'Brien's essays are to be found in Latin America Review of Books I (1974), F. Oxaal et al (eds), Beyond the Sociology of Development (London, 1975) and C. Abel and C.M. Lewis (eds) Latin America, Economic Imperialism and the State. The later draws upon a wide range of disciplinary and ideological perspectives: it considers the debates about the external connection from independence to the present. Widely acknowledged as the most perceptive dependency text is that of F.H. Cardoso and E. Faletto, Dependency and Development in Latin America (London, 1979). A less dense dependentista approach is S.J. and B.H. Stein, The Colonial Heritage of Latin America (New York, 1970). P. González Casanova, Imperialismo y liberación en América Latina (Mexico, 1978) and C.F.S. Cardoso and H. Pérez Brignoli, Historia económica de América Latina (Barcelona, 1979) have also received much acclaim. For the period studied, the principal exponent of the anti-imperialism/anti-dependency position is D.C.M. Platt. His main contributions are Trade, Finance and Politics in British Foreign Policy, 1815-1914 (Oxford, 1968) which has a world focus; Latin America and British Trade, 1806-1914 (London, 1972); and (ed) Business Imperialism, 1840-1930 (Oxford, 1977). He has also been published in many learned journals, notably the Economic History Review XVI (1968), XXVI (1973) and XXXIII (1980); Past and Present 39 (1968); Journal of Imperial and Commonwealth History II (1973); Latin American Research Review XV (1980).

For the independence period P.K. Liss, Atlantic Empires (Baltimore, 1983) presents a careful examination of contemporary issues and concepts. She also examines current approaches to the revolutionary struggles elaborated within the discourse on dependency. J.I. Domínguez, Insurrection or Loyalty (Cambridge, Mass., 1980) offers a revisionist critique of independence. For the early nineteenth century and beyond, an historical dimension to the ECLA development thesis, from which the dependency controversy in part emerged, is contained in C. Furtado, Economic Development of Latin America (Cambridge, 2nd ed. 1977) and O. Sunkul, O marco histórico do processo desenvolvimento/subdesenvolvimento (various editions). National examples of cepalista interpretations are A. Ferrer, The Argentine Economy (Berkeley, 1967), C. Furtado, The Economic Growth of Brazil (Berkeley, 1963) and A. Pinto S.C., Chile, una economía difícil (Santiago, 1966). These works do not address the imperialism/dependency debates directly but offer an alternative perspective. National studies directly challenging dependency or imperialism theses are J.C. Brown, A Socioeconomic History of Argentina 1776-1860 (Cambridge, 1979), C.F. Díaz Alejandro, Essays on the Economic History of the Argentine Republic (New Haven, 1970) and H.S. Ferns, Britain and Argentina in the Nineteenth Century (Oxford, 1960). For a contrast see R. Scalabrini Ortiz, Política Británica en el Río de la Plata (Buenos Aires, various editions). Fairly conventional marxist interpretations are provided by J.C. Mariátegui, 7 ensavos de interpretación de la realidad peruana (Lima, 1928), C. Prado Jr, História econômica do Brasil (Sao Paulo, 1953) and H. Ramírez Necochea, História del imperialismo en Chile (Santiago, 1970). Alternative views are expressed in R. Thorp and G. Bertram, Peru, 1890-1977 (London, 1978), and M.J. Mamalakis, The Growth and Structure of the Chilean Economy (New Haven, 1976). The former monograph is to some extent a response to dependency writings, the latter emerges from an attempt to elaborate a dynamic theory of growth which is non-(some would argue anti-)marxist while rejecting also conventional concepts of modernisation.


# Economic Penetration and the Scramble for Southern Africa


A short introduction is D. Denoon, Southern Africa since 1800 (2nd edit., Harlow, 1984). Thereafter the general reader might consult edit. M. Wilson and L. Thompson, The Oxford History of South Africa (2 vols., Oxford, 1969-75) and edit. J.E. Flint, The Cambridge History of Africa vol.5 (Cambridge, 1976). Three older books in the 'liberal' tradition cover South African history in detail until the 1880s: W.M. Macmillan, Bantu, Boer and Briton (London, 1929), J.S. Galbraith, Reluctant Empire (Berkeley, 1963) and C. de Kiewiet, The Imperial Factor in South Africa (Cambridge, 1937). The latter is one of the few books justly described as a 'classic'. For central Africa see edit. D. Birmingham and P. Martin, History of Central Africa (2 vols., Harlow, 1983). The nineteenth century slave trade is discussed in E.A. Alpers, Ivory and Slaves in East Central Africa (London, 1975) and in L. Vail and L. White, Capitalism and Colonialism in Mozambique (London, 1980). Much of the most important recent research has centred on the economic history of the African peoples of central and southern Africa. Two important collections of papers are P. Palmer and N. Parsons, The Roots of Rural Poverty (London, 1977) and S. Marks and A. Atmore, Economy and Society in pre-Industrial South Africa (Harlow, 1980). Also of major importance are C. Bundy, The Rise and Fall of the South African Peasantry (London, 1979) and W.G. Clarence-Smith, Slaves, Peasants and Capitalists in Southern Angola 1840-1926 (Cambridge, 1979). A reinterpretation of the 1870s and the origins of the Zulu War is contained in N. Etherington, 'Labour Supply and the Genesis of the South African Confederation in the 1870s', Journal of African History, 20, 1979, pp.235-253 and J. Guy, The Destruction of the Zulu Kingdom (Harlow, 1979). For the Portuguese colonies, see the books by Vail and White, and Clarence-Smith cited above and also M. Newitt, Portuguese Settlement on the Zambezi (Harlow, 1973) for Portugal's relations with the slavers, and R. Hammond, Portugal and Africa 1815-1910 (Stanford, 1966). The situation in the Indian Ocean is dealt with comprehensively in G.S. Graham, Great Britain in the Indian Ocean (Oxford, 1967) and the rivalries of the powers in Madagascar are described in P.M. Mutibwa, The Malagasy and the Europeans (Harlow, 1974). However, for revealing economic interpretations of events in Madagascar see the articles by G. Campbell, 'Labour and the Transport Problem in Imperial Madagascar 1810-1895', Journal of African History, 21, 1980, pp. 341-356 and 'Madagascar and the Slave Trade', ibid., 22, 1981, pp.203- 227. For the Comoro Islands and the French entrepreneurs there see M. Newitt, The Comoro Islands (Boulder, 1984). Diplomatic accounts of the scramble are too numerous to be included here, but a good modern account is D.M. Schreuder, The Scramble for Southern Africa, 1877-1895 (Cambridge, 1980).

# Russian Expansion into Central Asia

In addition to the works mentioned in the footnotes, the Russian conquest and subsequent history are covered in R.A. Pierce, Russian Central Asia 1867-1917 (Berkeley, 1960) and G. Wheeler, The Modern History of Soviet Central Asia (London, 1964). A brief survey of the khanates is contained in Mary Holdsworth, Turkestan in the Nineteenth Century (London, 1959) whilst the fullest study of Bokhara and Khiva is S. Becker, Russia's Protectorates in Central Asia (Cambridge, Mass., 1968). The standard anthropological study is Elizabeth Bacon, Central Asians under Russian Rule (Ithaca, N.Y., 1966). The most recent study of Anglo-Russian rivalry is D. Gillard, The Struggle for Asia, 1828-1914 (London, 1977) and a useful number of nineteenth-century British visitors to central Asia is F. Maclean, A Person from England (London, 1958). Amongst contemporary accounts of the area still of great value are the account of N.V. Khanikov, translated by C.A. de Bode, Bokhara: its Amir and People (London, 1845), Sir A. Burnes, Travels into Bukhara (3 vols., London, 1834), E. Schuyler, Turkistan (2 vols., London, 1876), J.A. MacGahan, Campaigning on the Oxus and the Fall of Khiva (New York, 1874) and G.N. Curzon, Russia in Central Asia in 1889 (London, 1889). The memoirs of Count Pahlen have been published in English, edit R.A. Pierce, Mission to Turkestan: the Memoirs of Count K.K. Pahlen, 1908-1909 (London, 1964).

# American Expansionism during the Gilded Age, 1865-98

I wish here to acknowledge my large debt to the works of many scholars who have written on this subject. A competent and useful survey to begin with is C.S. Campbell, The Transformation of American Foreign Relations, 1865-1900 (New York, 1976). An interesting and concise overview of the period is presented in A. Iriye, From Nationalism to Internationalism (Boston, 1977). On the historical debate, see E. May, American Imperialism (New York, 1968) and especially

R.L. Beisner, From the Old Diplomacy to the New, 1865-1900 (New York, 1975). For the economic interpretation of American diplomacy the seminal works are W.A. Williams, The Tragedy of American Diplomacy (New York, 1962) and W. LaFeber, The New Empire (Ithaca, 1963). On the politics of the McKinley years see the last chapter of W. Morgan, Unity and Culture: the United States, 1877-1900 (London, 1971). Diplomatic relations between the United States and Latin America are covered in J. Smith, Illusions of Conflict: Anglo-American Diplomacy toward Latin America, 1865-1896 (Pittsburgh, 1979) and for American attitudes to China see Marilyn B.Young, Rhetoric of Empire: American China Policy, 1895-1901 (Cambridge Mass., 1968). For the current state of the historical debate see the recent articles by J.A. Field, 'American Imperialism: the Worst Chapter in Almost any Book', American Historical Review, 83, 1978, and D.M. Pletcher, 'Rhetoric and Results: a Pragmatic View of American Economic Expansionism, 1865-1898', Diplomatic History, 5, 1981.

# BIOGRAPHICAL NOTES

Colin Lewis studied at Exeter as an undergraduate and took his PhD there in 1975. He has been a Lecturer in the Department of Economic History at the London School of Economics since 1970. He is author of British Railways in Argentina 1857-1914 and is co-editor with Christopher Abel of the forthcoming Economic Imperialism and Latin America.

Malyn Newitt taught at the University College of Rhodesia and is now Senior Lecturer in History at Exeter University. He is the author of Portuguese Settlement on the Zambesi, Portugal in Africa: the Last Hundred Years and The Comoro Islands.

Joseph Smith is a Lecturer in History at Exeter University. He is the author of Illusions of Conflict: Anglo-American Diplomacy Toward Latin America and has written widely on U.S. and British diplomacy towards Latin America. He is currently preparing a study of diplomatic relations between the United States and Brazil between 1889 and 1930.

Peter Morris is a Lecturer in History at Exeter University. He is the author of Eastern Europe since 1945 and has published widely on Russian, Central Asian and Iranian history.